AFRICA
THEN

AFRICA THEN

PHOTOGRAPHS

1840-1918

Edited and with an Introductory Text by

Nicolas Monti

Alfred A. Knopf
New York
1987

For my great-grandfather Leonard Moirand,
who went to Africa in 1911 as an officer
of the Foreign Legion, and my grandmother
Jeanne Marie Moirand-Bickert, who first
told me stories of Africa when
I was a little boy

THIS IS A BORZOI BOOK
PUBLISHED BY ALFRED A. KNOPF, INC.

Copyright © 1987 by Nicolas Monti

Library of Congress Cataloging-in-Publication Data

Africa then.

1. Africa—Description and travel—To 1900—Views.
2. Africa—Description and travel—1901–1950—Views.
I. Monti, Nicholas.
DT4.5.A37   1986   690'.23   86-45316
ISBN 0-394-55578-3

Manufactured in the United States of America
FIRST EDITION

CONTENTS

ACKNOWLEDGMENTS

In the course of producing this book I have become indebted to many different people and organizations. Appreciation is extended to the following institutions and individuals for making their collections available for the preparation of this book and the exhibition, and for services provided: Marchesa Camilla Salvago-Raggi; Jesse and Kate Hershkowitz; Touring Club Italiano, Milan; Collegio Internazionale della Consolata, Turin; Istituto Missioni Africane, Verona; Archivio Provinciale dei Capuccini, Milan; Istituto di Fotografia Alpina, Biella; Museum für Völkerkunde, Vienna; National Army Museum, London; Schomburg Center for Research in Black Culture, N.Y.P.L., New York.

Special thanks are extended to Francesca and Alessandra Pesci for their help in the initial research for the book. I am also most grateful to the following for the information they provided: Silvia Mazzola, Prof. Francesco Surdich, Dr. Andrew Roberts.

Many thanks for their support and special assistance go to the following individuals: Carole Kismaric; Michelangeo Lupo; Padre Sabatini, Collegio Internazionale della Consolata, Turin; Padre Zanotelli, Istituto Missioni Africane, Verona; Giovanna Rosselli, Touring Club Italiano, Milan; Padre Serafico Lorenzo, Archivio Provinciale dei Capuccini, Milan; Vittoria and Ludovico Sella, Istituto di Fotografia Alpina, Biella; Dr. Christian F. Feest, Museum für Völkerkunde, Vienna; Marion Harding, National Army Museum, London.

Acknowledgments

For years Massimo Basili, Giorgio Nicodemi, and, especially, Carla Manenti, all founding members of Centro Studi Monas Hierogliphica, have encouraged me in my interest in Africa and photography, and have given willingly of their time and expertise. For their support and advice, warm thanks are due to the people from ICP in New York who were involved at various stages in this project: Cornell Capa, Steve Rooney, Anne Doherty, Anne Hoy, Willis Hartshorn, Lisa Dirks, and William Ewing. For their reading of the manuscript, discussion of my ideas, and most helpful advice, I am much indebted to my father and to Paola Mola and Elena Elli. Many thanks to my partner in architecture, Giovanni Albera, for almost never complaining during all the time I spent in my African adventure.

I am also deeply grateful to my editor, Vicky Wilson, for her infinite patience with the author, and her great skill in pulling this book together.

And thanks above all to Anna Winand: were it not for the intelligence, faith, and passion that against all odds she brought to my cause, this book would never have been completed. I owe her a debt that is impossible to pay.

N.M.

AFRICA
THEN

INTRODUCTION

Another Place, Another Time

Like an archaeologist of a recent past, five years ago
I began to investigate fragments buried not so long
ago, belonging to an age whose history is still disturbing to us. As with many
of the early European travelers, for me Africa gradually became almost a
spiritual quest. Working through dusty photographs, maps, and documents, I
did my best to acquire a thorough knowledge of the continent and its people,
of its beauty and singularity.

Collecting is in a way very similar to hunting; the search for the object can
be as satisfying as its discovery. Very rarely did I collect something I did not
like or that did not interest me, however important it might have been from
other points of view. I began with Italian photographic collections, and then
looked through the archives of the European nations that had the strongest ties
with the African continent during the colonial period. And finally I looked
through African archives.

Photographic documentation on Africa turned out to be extremely scattered. I found more material in natural history and science museums than in
fine arts museums. There were photographs in the archives of societies, in
ministries that were closed when the colonies became independent, and in
former colonial companies. Sometimes, photographs were found through a
detective-like investigation that began with a newspaper clipping decades old.
Most collections were unclassified, uncatalogued, and neglected in dusty base-
ments.

The process of compiling a list of the existing collections and checking their condition, when the latest available information typically dated back thirty years, was slow and difficult. Luckily, quite a few individuals extended their support to the project; they include museum staff, history and art scholars, journalists and writers, corporation officials, private collectors and world travelers, members of the diplomatic corps and former officers in the colonial service, and friends. Contacts with Western and African scholars in very different disciplines ranging from anthropology to art history have been invaluable for a greater understanding of the images and how they relate to the general historical and cultural background. With a few exceptions, the photographs selected here have been reproduced only in publications issued at the time they were made.

The ethnographic portrait fascinated me: front-view, rear, profile, three-quarters, powerful muscles and extraordinary scars, heavy breasts and fantastic hair styles, hordes of ferocious warriors and regiments of provocative Venuses. At a certain stage, however, while selecting the photographs, I was overcome by increasing doubts. Wasn't I actually using the same criteria in my choice that had influenced the photographer? Wasn't I conditioned by the exoticism and the picturesque aspects that were lurking in those maps and documents yellowed with age, knowing that they had me under their spell?

A balanced relationship between the aesthetic values and the capacity of documenting Africa as it was at the time, presented a problem. That is also why I have included photographs by obscure photographers as well as professionals. I have been careful to discard contemporary fakes (scenes picturing African subjects but not actually photographed in Africa) except a few which I included because they evoke with particular effectiveness certain aspects of nineteenth-century customs.

Today Africa is no longer on the fringes of the known world. Its civilizations are changing, new currents are stimulating its soul. Its people are struggling to become part of the modern world without losing the lasting values of their cultural heritage.

The overturning of all established social structures, the unnatural bringing together of peoples who could achieve fulfillment only within the security of their own social environment and the landscapes glorified by their forefathers, resulted in fearful changes. "The empires of our time were short-lived, but they have altered the world forever; their passing away was their least significant feature."[1]

Political and economic colonization put an end to the age-old isolation of the continent; it opened Africa to the world and the world to Africa. We have not always had the same past, but we shall inevitably share a common future.

There is no single way to look at and characterize Africa, because it is too big, complex, and ever changing, even over a comparatively short period of time, to be encapsulated in any one vision or one single exhibition.

The aim of this book is to show some of the motives that formed the Romantic myth in which the European bourgeoisie tried for the last time to manifest two opposing values: freedom and power. These photographs reflect the attraction of the unknown, of the unseizable grandeur of the scenery, the boundless beauty and also the fierceness of nature associated with the fascination exerted by the African woman's sexuality/sensuality. On the other hand, they also reveal the violence of power, the pleasure of possession, the arrogance of a culture that denied and destroyed others it saw as different, the sadism of subjugation, the thirst for profit. "The Europeans wanted gold and slaves, like everybody else," writes V. S. Naipaul, "but at the same time they wanted statues put up to themselves as people who had done good things for the slaves. Being an intelligent and energetic people, and at the peak of their power, they could express both sides of their civilization; and they got the slaves and the statues."[2]

The conquest of a continent—the subject was grand-scale enough: the clash of cultures, the struggle between future and past, progress and reaction, and, indeed, even good and evil. Truly the stage was large and varied enough to accommodate vast events of far-reaching and incalculable consequences. Drama included a most incredible nature in sublime and exotic forms, and certainly there were also plenty of heroes and villains.

The bourgeois, deprived of their social status by the omnipotence of the multinational corporations, remain in the present "massification" only a reminiscence of the past. But this memory stays alive and active in the generations who regain their lost pride by identifying themselves with individual heroes of the times gone and by adopting, in disguise, certain fashion trends of the past. This may explain the recent interest in nineteenth-century Africa and its glorification by the entertainment media in their epics of the colonial adventure.

Advertisements, stores specializing in colonial apparel, best-sellers such as Isak Dinesen's *Out of Africa,* and the Oscar-winning movie based upon it, such films as *Indiana Jones*—these are the sources where the bourgeoisie can find, even if under the protective veil of irony, the values and myths of its class.

The form of this myth and the ways of its definition are displayed by the precious photographic sources here presented. The image of this history that the Europeans wanted to record is shown side by side with those elements beyond their control (as fixed by the camera lenses). Such features, now, a century later, give these images extraordinary documentary value.

That is why the photographs should be analytically seen as an ingenious effort to go beyond simple visual recording of the things that could be observed, and to influence our perception of reality, thus creating an image of Africa that, in part, never existed.

Photography in Africa

Beginning in the seventeenth century, Europe had regular commercial relations with the distant continent of Africa. "The Companies of the Indies" founded the first trading posts; diplomatic relations were established with local sovereigns; and a vast trade in slaves and goods developed. Yet, in 1837, when Victoria ascended to the British throne, Africa—its peoples and cultures—was for Westerners still largely a *terra incognita*. Only her coasts, her southern tip, and the Muslim potentates of the North were relatively well known.

The invention of photography coincided with the true beginnings of the European presence in Africa and after November 1839 enabled the documentation of the ever more decisive European incursion into Africa's politics, economy, religion, and culture, and transmitted to the outside world its first view of the immense and indecipherable African continent.

The discoveries and superhuman efforts of the explorers, the secrets of the harems, the dark jungles and incandescent deserts, the transformation of entire peoples and of immense territories under the yoke of laws and governments unknown to them, could now be documented in precise and reproducible images. This view of Africa transmitted by photography, however, never was nor could be impartial; it was above all a Western interpretation, particularly rich in fantastic ideas.

The Romantic passion for the East, propagated in the poems of Hugo, Byron, Coleridge, and Gérard de Nerval, in the novels of Flaubert, in the accounts of Kinglake's travels; the taste for the exotic and fantastic inspired by the first translations of *A Thousand and One Nights,* which were inaccurate but rich in color; the largely imaginary but extremely effective evocations of painters such as Delacroix in *The Death of Sardanapalus* or Ingres in *The Grand Odalisque*—all played important parts in impelling the pioneers of photography Eastward. The seductive mystery of ancient bygone civilizations; the subtle melancholy of architecture in ruins, biblical memories, and mystical aspirations; knightly medieval legends, romantic and sentimental adventures of nomad warriors, of blood-shedding sultans and pashas, of sweet and easy almahs—all share in creating this Africa, which, as Hugo wrote, is an image, a thought, a dream more than a real land. Intuitions and passions crystallized and were conveyed in the best part of the photographers' work and were, for a long time, a product much sought by the cultivated and attentive Western connoisseur.

On January 9, 1839, before an enthusiastic audience, during a session of the French Academy of Science, the physicist François Arago revealed Daguerre's invention. Within a few months the new technique spread rapidly throughout most parts of Europe and beyond. Photography reached Africa on November 6, 1839, with the first daguerreotypes on Egyptian antiquity by the orientalist painter Horace Vernet. Ten years later, another amateur, the writer Maxime du Camp, brought back from the continent the first reproducible images.

At first, travel and exploration photography seems to have been done only by amateurs: painters, writers, men of science (archaeologists, anthropologists, geographers, botanists)—very often adventurers who embodied the qualities and flaws of all these categories. The enthusiasm close to obsession and courage close to madness of these pioneers were sufficient to deal with the difficulties and dangers, similar to those faced by the explorer and missionary who came just before them, but compounded by the typical professional risks of the photographer. At first, most photographic work was necessarily scenic and monumental photography. Besides all the bulky and heavy equipment, to the usual technical limitations (for example, slow shutter speeds) were added those caused by a hostile environment, which had a deleterious effect both on the equipment and on its operator, to such a point that in many cases a drawing of the subject was still preferred. Every noteworthy African expedition, besides its usual supply of watches, compasses, thermometers and sextants, was burdened with a collection of cameras, which, however, were used very little and with little

success. In fact "the severity of the climate soon made work tiring and unhealthy."[3] Accompanying Speke on his 1860–63 expedition to the sources of the Nile, James Augustus Grant, after a successful photographic effort at Zanzibar, could not obtain, for the rest of the trip, any satisfactory results and was forced to give up the camera for the sketching pad. Also Charles Livingstone, the official photographer of the 1858 Zambesi expedition and brother of the famous explorer, proved to be totally unable—partly owing to his ignorance of chemical processes and photographic technique—to produce "something having a faint likeness to a picture."

The struggle often disproportionate to the results makes the photographer's achievements all the more remarkable and highlights the skill and determination needed by the operator in almost impossible circumstances.

The success of a shot was never certain, and very often the photographer, when telling about his trip, was amazed at his own success. In 1857, the English photographer Francis Frith in Egypt used the wet collodion process, which required coating the glass plate, exposing it, and developing the resulting photograph before the film dried. He wrote about the difficulty and unpredictability of working with this process in the desert, in an airless tent at 115°F and higher, in an atmosphere full of ether fumes. "Now in a smothering little tent, with my collodion fizzing-boiling up all over the glass the instant that it touched and, again, pushing my way backward, upon my hands and knees, into a damp slimy rocktomb to manipulate, it is truly marvelous that the results should be presentable at all."

Any traveler who wanted to undertake a photographic campaign in those years had to face almost impossible hardships. Common and pervasive problems were heat and humidity, the formation of mold and dust, the bad quality of chemicals, and a lack of sufficient distilled water. Moreover, the collodion (a chemical used by early photographers) almost always had to be smuggled in: steamship lines refused to transport it, because its active

6

ingredient was also the explosive ingredient of a special type of gunpowder.★ Over time, however, equipment was refined and experience accumulated. The human component could finally be inserted into the images, and an interest developed in photographically documenting the customs and traditions of the local people.

It must be noted, however, that except for the very first photographs of Egypt, the presence of the human image rarely offered the possibility of measuring distance and object, but it was included in scenic compositions for artistic purposes. For a long time the African man did not constitute an independent subject except in so-called anthropological studies. We can thus distinguish photographs in which an architectural feature dominates, photographs in which nature and the scenery are of principal interest, and finally photographs of the people, nearly always consciously composed, to which, but only much later, the snapshot was added.

At first, photographers followed the esthetic rules and graphic conventions of contemporary painting. During the eighteenth century, professional artists had often been part of exploratory expeditions and had pioneered in formulating and applying artistic theories that conditioned the work of their direct successors. Thus, at the beginning of the 1800s, existing African iconography put a heavy burden on the choice of the subject and on the ways of representation of the first photographers, who did their best to reconstruct the true Africa in such a way as to make it as similar as possible to the Africa imagined by the previous generation of European artists. Particularly strong was the influence of the theories of the "Picturesque," by Gilpin,[4] shown especially in perspective interpretation and reconstruction of the "typical" life of the native.

Some of these photographs betray an underlying racism and paternalism in their often sophisticated compo-

★ In 1846 C. F. Schonbein invented a process for making guncotton, intending to use it as an explosive agent in firearms. Guncotton and hen's eggs were the raw materials of the process used to obtain collodion and albumen.

sitions. Today they appear as the vestiges of an era in which Europe sincerely believed in the legitimacy of its claim to universal civilization. Many other works convey an understanding of the continent and its inhabitants, and one discovers with a certain surprise that photography in Africa, even though it remains rather faithful to the cultural trends of the period, often presents itself in an original and modern way, sometimes with surprising intuition, if compared to contemporary photographic production in Europe.

Photographic documents taken by native photographers are relatively rare. In North Africa the Aniconic mandate, that is, the Koranic prohibition against realistic images, was strictly observed and was thus a strong deterrent. For a long time in Muslim countries, the belief persisted that the reproduction of human features was an offense to God—from which followed an understandably negative view of the photograph, the iconic image par excellence. It is enough to remember that when photography arrived in Egypt in 1839, the Khedive exclaimed, "This is the work of the Devil!" Most photographers, therefore, were either Westerners or Christian Armenians. The latter were particularly active in Egypt, and photographers like Sébah (originally from Constantinople), Lekegian (who worked for the British Occupational Forces), Zangaki, and Peridis, collected vast files of landscapes and genre scenes. Also the Abdullah brothers, photographers at the court of the Turkish sultans, were Armenians who converted to Islam after receiving the Imperial Commission. If this was the situation in the more westernized and richest part of the continent, in Black Africa the birth of native photography was impeded by more serious cultural and economic problems. As late as 1896, an Abyssinian nobleman, speaking of photographer Edoardo Ximenes and his camera, exclaimed threateningly: "This man has too much in his camera and I think it's enough. Does this man want to take away the whole country?"

It is certain that native photographers, usually blacks converted to Christianity and educated in Europe, were active in some of the oldest colonies. Names often are misleading and it is hard to guess what color of skin is hidden behind an English, French, or Portuguese family name. The yearbooks of the colonies do not mention the race of the local society's prominent members, but they do sometimes publish their photographic portraits and it may come as a surprise to discover that some of the local photographers were black Africans. *The Red Book of West Africa* printed portraits by George S. A. Da Costa, active in Lagos, Nigeria, beginning in 1895; N. Walwin Holm started his business in Accra, Ghana, as early as 1883 and was in 1897 the first photographer of the colony to be enrolled as a member of the Royal Photographic Society of Great Britain; and the Lisk-Carew brothers established, in 1905, the most fashionable photographic studio in Freetown, Sierra Leone.

Yet the authorities who commissioned and financed a good part of the first photographic campaigns were, it seems, aware of the risk of "natives" getting possession of this means of expression and using it as an instrument of subversion by showing the true conditions of their people, rather than a celebrative view of colonialism or an easy and misleading exoticism. And so the illustration of Africa's social reality was until independence mostly the work of European photographers. The colonial authorities sometimes even blocked the diffusion of some photographic materials in the colonies. This happened, for instance, with photographs of sovereigns sent into exile by the colonial powers or in Muslim countries with the photographs of Arab women appearing in unseemly postures. But the dissemination and success of such materials were still guaranteed in Europe. There an avid public looked greedily to Africa for adventures (mediated through stories, photographs, and cinema), which imbued them with heroism and fanaticism, drama and delirium, passion and eroticism. Certainly the exoticism of some colonial material, emphasizing the clichés that for a long time hid an imperialist mechanism, greatly contributed to the European's sense of his own superiority.

Whatever the consequences, through these images an immense public looked for and discovered a colored Africa largely of its own making: a sadistic, violent, decadent, mysterious, languid, passionate world, which totally deranged the senses. The armchair hero became a devotee and expert on the secrets of harems, on the dark rites of wild cannibals, on barbaric hunts and geographic mysteries. Ottomans covered with heavy Persian carpets and Chinese silks, tea trays inlaid with ivory and mother-of-pearl began to appear in the drawing rooms of bourgeois homes. With the help of the carpet weaver, with some sparkling scimitars and hunting trophies of animals that luckily nobody in the family had seen alive, one strove to give style and lyrical meaning to the dull reality of everyday life. People of lesser means consoled themselves by swelling with increasing enthusiasm the ranks of missionaries and soldiers who went off to be killed in exquisitely exotic ways far from home.

The time was right to try to make a profit from the image, especially the photographic, of travels and exotic subjects. The first person who tried to industrialize and commercialize the photographic image was a French entrepreneur, Blanquart-Evrard, himself a renowned amateur photographer. Between 1852 and 1855 he published the first photo albums, mainly with travel pictures, particularly of Egypt. Besides the albums of Maxime du Camp, John B. Greene, and V. G. Maunier, he reproduced several "keepsakes," which gathered photographs of several artists.

The most fashionable subject for a long time remained the land of the Pharaohs and Biblical sites. The albums of Félix Teynard (1853–58), Louis de Clercq (1859–60), Aymard de Banville (1865), and Félix Bonfils's first edition (1872) belong to the same period. Most prolific of all, however, was unquestionably the Englishman Francis Frith. His documentation of Egypt and the Holy Land had, in a country imbued with Biblical influences like Great Britain, an enormous success. His albums were printed in editions of 2,000: altogether 150,000 original mounted and bound photographs. Drawing-room adventurers constituted the rich and satisfied clientele of these works, always ready to spend in hard cash what they saved in danger and discomfort.

Photographic albums, almost always published in installments, often fetched fabulous prices; for example, the *dessins photographiques* of Du Camp cost 500 gold francs. We can get a clearer idea of the prices involved if we consider that going up the Nile around 1860 on a boat hired for one month, accompanied by a dragoman (a sort of native guide and butler), a cook, and a waiter, with all the necessities for a pleasant, if not comfortable, trip, cost around 56 pounds per person[5]; compare this with the price of 53 pounds for the illustrated Bible by Frith, on sale in 1862. Romantic views of the desert and Arabian fantasies adorned bourgeois homes; photographs of lovely exotic women in various stages of nudity and of sophisticated tortures contributed to the attractions of the rich bachelor's library. Many of these same people liked to be portrayed in heroic poses in slightly too rich Oriental dress, or in the uniform of the fully equipped Africanist.

While we have records of widespread activity in Egypt and in the French North African possessions beginning in the early 1840s, south of the desert photography was practically absent in those early days until one reached the southern tip of the continent, where, in Port Elizabeth, the earliest recorded daguerreotype studio was opened by a Frenchman, Jules Léger, in 1846. Because of the sparseness of the population, pioneer photographers could not afford to stay in just one place, but had to become itinerants, journeying constantly from town to town, to earn a living. Very little documentation of this "heroic" period survives; only brief entries in commercial almanacs and small-town newspaper reports and advertisements—often suggesting the usually precarious financial status of these pioneers—remain to help trace their activities and whereabouts. In 1849, the first recorded calotype photographer, A. W. Roghe from Frankfurt, established his studio in South Africa, but the next year he left for India and Burma. In 1850, John Paul arrived in Cape Town and somehow managed to work in the colony for six years,

but finally he too had to give up and leave for India, where he committed suicide in 1862.

By midcentury, the growing numbers of European colonists offered photographers a more stable and steady clientele, and as a consequence, their record of the life of the major settlements becomes fuller and more accurate. Even so, in the whole period between 1846 and 1870, only 48 professional firms are recorded as operating in Cape Town, one of the most populous cities of the continent, and one has only to compare this figure with the 43 photographers advertising their services in Melbourne in the year 1867 alone.

In fact photography as a profession was rarely remunerative. Photographers often had to supplement their photographic trade with more or less related activities. Lehnert & Landrock were also printers, and later publishers, in Tunis and Germany; like many others, J. M. Lazarus, who opened a studio in Lourenço Marques in the late 1880s, advertised three lines of business—photography, bookselling, and stationery; in Accra, the Lisk-Carew brothers advertised their business as "Photographers, Importers of Photographic Materials, Stationery, Toys, Fancy Goods, etc."

Between 1860 and 1880, the market for travel photography increased tremendously. The growing safety of many overseas countries, most of them still theoretically independent, but by now tied to disastrous alliances or humiliating protectorates, allowed the creation of large photographic companies outside Europe, such as in British East Africa and Zanzibar (Gomes, Coutinho, Young), in Egypt (Sébah, Langaki, Beato, Lekegian, Fiorillo), in Tunisia (Lehnert & Landrock), in Abyssinia (Naretti, Nicotra), in Angola (Moraes), in Mozambique (Lazarus, Pereira), in South Africa (Gros, Harris). Since 1863, Samuel Bourne could claim in *The British Journal of Photography,* "there is now scarcely a nook or corner, a glen, a valley, a mountain, much less a country, on the face of the globe which the penetrating eye of the camera has not searched, or where the fumes of poor Archer's collodion have not risen through the hot or freezing atmosphere."[6]

The increasing number of permanent photographic studios documenting the growth and potential of the various colonies found, from the early 1850s on, their largest public when some of their work was included in the great international exhibitions. On the occasion of the 1855 Paris International Exhibition, Ernest Lacan had celebrated the way in which photography had "sailed the oceans, conquered the mountains, crossed the continents," thus acquainting the public with remote places that had so far been known only through drawings and etchings. Of course, much material was adapted for publication in contemporary newspapers and magazines, or reproduced in book form in the personal accounts and memoirs of the protagonists. Moraes took photographs showing the development of the Great Fazendas in Angola and published between 1885 and 1888 the four-volume *Africa Occidental: Album photographico e descriptivo;* Robert Harris, in his *South Africa Illustrated in a Series of One Hundred and Four Permanent Photographs,* published in 1888, focused on the mineral wealth and exploitation of the land, and was persuaded that he had here produced "a book not only of very general interest, but one which may be found of considerable value to those interested in the future welfare of South Africa."

Many combined photography and text in an effort to highlight the beneficial aspects of the colonial endeavor. One of the most significant of such publications was *The Queen's Empire* (1897), featuring 300 half-tone prints with extensive captions and an introduction by H. O. Arnold-Foster, M.P. The volume conveyed an idealized picture of a British Empire where, "with all the variety and all the novelty there is yet, happily, one bond of union, one mark of uniformity. In every part of the Empire we shall find some trace of the work which Britain is doing throughout the world—the work of civilising, of governing, of protecting life and property, and of extending the benefits of trade and commerce."

Not only was the growth of commerce and agriculture documented, but also great engineering feats, particularly railways, which to the Victorian mind were the vanguard of the onward march of civilization. William D. Young, who came to East Africa in the late 1890s after working as a railway photographer in eastern India, was the official photographer of the Uganda Railway. While most of his vast number of pictures recorded purely technical aspects of the construction of the line, some were impressive enough to be advertised as "camera pictures from Mombasa to Victoria Nyanza," and sold commercially.

Even though the adventurous spirit never disappeared completely, the quality of commercial production diminished rapidly. Important archives of photographic plates passed from one company to the other and were plagiarized; the new owner hurriedly erased the name of the original one and engraved his own name. Nevertheless this was not the end of fine photography in Africa. Once more amateurs stepped in for professionals.

After 1880 the introduction on the market of smaller cameras and fast films substantially reduced both the difficulty of photography and the amount of equipment needed. The role of the photographer changed, as did the sort of picture taken. The easiness of modern photography has meant that almost any event can be captured on film without the formalities of rigid posing and elaborate setting up that characterize much nineteenth-century work. What this has meant in terms of photographic standards may be arguable, as amateurs often lack the technical skills of the professional photographer, but the change is reflected in the enormous mass of pictures taken and the wide variety of backgrounds of those who are now in a position to use the camera. "Now that industry has invented small-size, easy-to-carry cameras with dry coated plates, the equipment of any proper expedition should not be without such a useful device."[7]

This opinion must have been shared by the Royal Geographical Society, which appointed John Thomson as instructor of photography in order to teach African explorers to bring back from their travels accurate visual records. These ideas had already been expressed in the past but turned up again each time a new technical discovery made the photographer's work easier. And so, in 1846, commenting favorably on the greater ease and simplicity of handling calotype, the *Art Union Journal* suggested some practical uses of photography. It asserted that the camera should "be henceforth an indispensable accompaniment to all exploring expeditions," and argued that "by taking sun pictures of striking natural objects the explorer will be able to define his route with such accuracy as greatly to abbreviate the toils and diminish the dangers of those who may follow in his track"[8] and that in exploring the African waterways, localities "fearfully infected by miasmata and malaria" might be recognized and avoided.

Until then the presence of a photographer on the right spot at the right moment, and the survival of his pictures, had often been a matter of pure chance. Various events of great historical importance, owing to the remoteness of their locations, took place without a photographer anywhere near to document them (though it may also be the case that the significance of a given event was not appreciated at the time). From 1880 onward, however, thanks to the simplicity of the new photographic processes, it has hardly ever occurred that events of a certain importance were not recorded. The potential of photography as a documenter of European achievements was now well understood, and the photographer's indiscreet and personal glance offers us a view of the event while it is taking place. There are countless examples—for instance, the work of William Ellerton Fry with the Pioneer Column into Mashonaland in 1890; of Ernest Gedge with the Imperial British East Africa Company caravan to Uganda in 1888–90; or of N. Walwin Holm, who was commissioned by Major G. C. Denton to photograph in 1891 the raising of the British flag in the territories of Igbessa, Ado, Ilaro, and Pokra in Nigeria. Scientists, soldiers, journalists, mountain climbers, tourists, and rich idle travelers enthusiastically went on the chase for the unusual, the as yet undiscovered reality, and the surrealistic.

Photography in Africa is a monument to a lost, bloody, imperialist, but nevertheless exciting and even heroic period—a memory of the past, and an image of the present and the future, focusing on the end of an era to suggest the shape of things to come; the last untouched wilderness overcome by men of action with almost biblical results; the white man equipped with a child's dreams and a man's courage, against enormous odds, opening and conquering a new continent, competing for the "heathen" souls of the natives; ending within a few decades nature's patterns, cycles, balances. As this period came to an end, the equilibrium and harmony of a whole continent was irretrievably altered. By 1918, the dividing up of the continent was concluded and administrative colonialism in its definitive form began. Entire peoples had involuntarily become "the white man's burden" and were now subject to the will of the colonial state. Photographers had been there to document this dramatic transformation.

I

FALSE DAWN

EXPLORATION
AND DISCOVERY

The subdivision into periods tends to reduce histor-ical developments into well-defined stages, which in our case would lead us from the age of exploration to colonialism and, less than a century later, to decolonization. Adopting these subdivisions, which are often arbitrary, involves the inevitable risk of losing sight of the continuity that links each period in which not only are the various problems interdependent but the various codes (political, esthetic, literary, ethnographical) are almost impossible to separate. European culture exports and projects its values—and obviously also its superstitions—into the cultures of the colonized countries and strengthens and focuses its own identity by comparing and thus differen-tiating itself from Africa—an Africa perceived as a projection of Europe itself, only slightly different, fascinating although inferior, because of its presumed lack of evolution.

The great European cultures were deeply involved with the colonial phe-nomenon in a relationship of reciprocal exchange (not in a one-way flow, as many people like to think) and still are influenced by this experience. The great variety of interpretations and tendencies in interpreting this phenomenon con-firms the importance of this experience in European thought. The concept of exoticism presupposes the will to assert a difference; it arises from dissatisfac-tion with one's own way of life. It means refusal of the norm and research into the marginal.

In those days, undertaking a trip beyond Europe still meant abandoning one's own country for very long periods. It was quite normal to establish oneself for some time in one of the countries visited, sometimes for a few months or even for several years. In so doing, photographers were following the example of painters of the previous generation, for whom Algeria and Turkey had replaced Italy in the traditional grand tour. In Mediterranean Africa and the Near East, photographers found it hard to resist the temptation to "go native," to grow a beard and dress in local attire, exchanging their top hats for large turbans and their clumsy boots for soft babouches. Many of them settled in Arab quarters, where they lived sometimes modestly, but more often with true oriental pomp: they bought slaves, smoked hashish, and, far removed from the conventions of their time, were able to indulge freely tastes and habits that were unacceptable in their motherlands; sometimes they even converted to Islam.

The infringement of a whole series of social, religious, and sexual conventions reveals the impelling desire to modify one's habitual identity, in order to assume the restless and disquieting masks of the unknown, diversity, and exoticism. It was an extreme reaction to the type of equalizing frame of mind that was establishing itself more and more in the West. The "call of adventure," an expression used in romantic literature, or, even better, the motive of "crossing the threshold of civilization" was very well outlined by de Maupassant in his preface to *Au Soleil,* when he compares the journey to "a kind of door through which one leaves known reality to penetrate another, unexplored and dreamlike reality," adding: "I felt attracted to Africa by an overwhelming need."

This crossing of the threshold of civilization was sometimes experienced as a dizziness in which the white man, transgressing the values of bourgeois society, loses for a moment (or forever) the control of reason and enters a world of dreams. The misery and splendor of passions, violence, adventure, and even death were eagerly accepted in the attempt to unveil and free the secret potentialities of one's being.

Once the great "general ideas" have failed and been abandoned, salvation can come only individually. The lyrical outburst of sentiments becomes actual decision, gesture, and action. Poetry is transformed into practice. From Rimbaud to Gauguin, the examples abound. The alienation of many outstanding intellectuals from the political and cultural positions of their class of origin thus contributes to initiate a form of protest mainly expressed by actual flight. The polemics against the "bourgeois" initiated by the first Romanticist, more as a pose than out of real conviction, evolved, mainly from the 1870s onward, into a radical attitude for increasingly precise and bitter reasons. A modern society in which the old differences between social classes had been replaced by a dull bureaucratic and productive uniformity led many sensitive individuals to a rejection both of the new political regime and of the law of profit which inevitably brought the destruction of the values of honor and individual force. Such individuals proposed to recover these values through exotic escape from the hypocrisy and corruption of contemporary society.

What a dismal existence am I leading under this absurd climate and these senseless conditions! How boring! What a stupid life! What am I doing here? And what would I be looking for elsewhere? If I had the means to travel without having to stop and to work for a living, I would not be seen for more than two months in the same place. The world is full of wonderful places.[1]

Oh, to escape, to leave! to escape from the old familiar places, from people, from the repetition of the same old movements at the same hours and, above all, from the same old thoughts! When one is so sick and tired as to cry from morning till night, tired to the point of not wanting to get up for a glass of water, fed up with friendly faces that one has seen so often they are irritating, fed up with the obnoxious and placid neighbors, with all the familiar and tedious things, with one's home, one's street . . . , tired of a too faithful dog, of the eternal stains on the draperies, of the regularity of rest and sleeping in the same bed, of every action repeated every day, fed up with oneself, with the narrow circle in which one's thoughts are running, fed up with one's own face in the mirror, with one's grimaces while shaving or combing one's hair, one has to leave, enter a new and varying life.[2]

The decisive choice of an adopted country became the alternative option to a global choice of culture. This decision had its roots in two related factors: a lack of confidence in the validity or value of the exact sciences and of the notion of a "progressive human destiny," and a strong rejection of the growing cultural, social, and political homogeneity orchestrated in Europe by the triumphant bourgeoisie, now the true hegemonic class. "Here everyone wears a uniform, grey overcoat, hat or cap. . . . Here everything is foreseen, regulated and numbered; there are laws for everything and regulations for everybody, so that the lowest poor person, pedlar, or barber's boy has the same rights in life as an intelligent and resolute young man."[3]

The logical consequence was a clash between the individual affirming the power of his will and a mediocre, prosaic society which lacked ideals and was dominated by the herd instinct, by the chains of alienating work, by moral wretchedness.

From Egypt, where he stayed six months with his photographer/painter friend Maxime du Camp, Gustave Flaubert wrote:

If in France everything is in the same poor state as it was when I left, if the bourgeois are still so utterly inept and public opinion so cowardly, in other words if the general daily fare is still emanating such a dirty, greasy smell, I do not miss anything; on the contrary, whether everything turns out for the best or the worst, I do not want any part of the general cake. I avoid the crowds in order to save my elbows.[4]

Far from the productive and legal machinery of the new industrial Europe, in lands not yet touched by the stinking egalitarian wind blowing from the West, it was still possible to accomplish a life's dream. This dream, projected toward an idealized past, was conceived as an esthetic, anti-modern, and anti-scientific enterprise, an attempt to re-create a time when "faith, sublime dream,

and noble personal daring established the force of the nations."[5] Loti was grateful to the Sultan of Morocco for being handsome, for wanting neither Parliament nor press nor railways nor roads, and for riding superb horses. He admired his noble and calm contempt for the unrest of modern times and shared his belief that an ancestral faith, which still created martyrs and prophets, was a treasure worth safeguarding and a consolation to men in the hour of their death. The rejection of contemporary Europe created a distortion of historical consciousness; present times were experienced in a spirit of nostalgia, as a quest for an idealized past that might have had very different outcomes, from Winckelmann's conception of antiquity to Rousseau's of nature.

Intellectuals were not alone in such views: An endless stream of adventurers, soldiers, merchants, and missionaries left the old continent in only a few decades. It was a general escape from a Europe too small and too petty, an escape to elevated risks and passions, to a bigger land, to a continent with mountains miles high and rivers so wide the other bank could not be seen, to journeys that lasted years and consumed lives. Africa and the Orient were the only parts of the world where a strong and courageous man still had the possibility of becoming a hero.

Rimbaud was nineteen years old when he abandoned art with his global refusal of the vulgarity and hypocrisy of a society and an intolerable way of life. In Africa he recognized a land of escape and, above all, of rebirth: "I shall come back with steel limbs, dark skin, furious eyes; because of the mask I will wear, I will be considered of a strong race. I will have gold, be lazy and brutal . . . I will participate in politics. Saved."[6]

This attitude justified the often desperate attempt, impelled in part by society itself, to save on other shores a rich cultural store that could not be sacrificed to the prevailing beliefs. European man transferred his own repressed desires "elsewhere," where fiction and marvel met with reality. At the physical and cultural borders of Europe, at the edges of history and civilization, he found again through exoticism the capacity to experiment with the fantastic and therefore to create, in an artistic sense as well; to discover and feel unknown and forbidden temptations. He found also a physical place where it was possible to give new life to ancient myths and to form new ones.

What the early missionaries had gazed upon with freshness and wonder, explorers would soon conquer and name, geographers would explain, often incorrectly, and the tourist would one day take for granted. Lone men of courage and initiative overcame the land with a curious mixture of altruism, practicality, and political expediency.

. . . the bizarre obstinacy of that desire made them defy death in a thousand shapes; the unknown seas, the loathsome and strange diseases; wounds, captivity, hunger, pestilence, and despair. It made them great! By heavens! it made them heroic; and made them pathetic, too, in their craving to confront and engage death, so implacably levying its toll on young and old. . . . And indeed those who adventured their persons and lives risked all they had for a slender reward. They left their bones to lie bleaching on distant shores, so that wealth might flow to the living at home. To us, their less-tried successors, they appear magnified, not as agents of trade, but as instruments of a recorded destiny, pushing out into the unknown in obedience to an inward voice, to an impulse beating in the blood, to a dream of the future. They were wonderful; and it must be owned they were ready for the wonderful. They recorded it complacently in their sufferings, in the aspect of the seas, in the customs of strange nations, in the glory of splendid rulers.[7]

And the artist being "there," side by side with the explorer and the builder of empires, certified his heroic status. By vanquishing so many physical and psychological obstacles on his way, he became the hero of his own journey to the antipodes of civilization, in search of a new world. However, no one let himself be deceived: it was only a matter of time before this world too was bound to disappear, "inevitably dragged into the modern universal banality."[8]

The frequently desperate attempts to save on distant shores social, cultural, and human values no longer compatible with prevailing conventions were, in part, managed by society itself, which thus found a way of getting rid of, and at times putting to use, its deviants. Moreover, it is clear that all these instances were bound to be suffocated in the hour of triumph of the colonial system, which sanctioned the disappearance of those zones where it had been possible to exist in full freedom. At that time the mechanism of reconverting any wealth of imagination into merchandise and the expansion on a planetary scale of the imperatives of Western production were, in fact, already operating everywhere. Maybe it would have been preferable, right from the start, not to take the risk of leaving and thus discovering a reality rather different from what was expected. Some had never had any doubts. Paul Valéry wrote, "One should acquire knowledge only through pictures, narration or reading . . . only of the least erudite, most inexact and even the most confusing kind. That is how you collect good material for dreams. A mixture of space and time is needed, of pseudo-truths and false certainties, of infinite details and coarsely broad views. That is how you find the Orient of the mind."[9]

There is no doubt that exoticism itself is inseparable from the sense of guilt felt for all that which was destroyed, inadvertently or intentionally. In Africa, as everywhere else outside Europe, destruction and Western civilization were linked. In an apparent paradox, the overwhelming action of European civilization defiled and, in the end, obliterated that very past and nature that it slowly, but often intelligently and with enthusiasm, sought to appreciate and reassess. Europeans realized the great damage they were causing only when it was much too late. But this awareness would not in any case have sufficed to halt the onward course of events: the victorious march of progress was part of history and could not be arrested.

The white man comes: everything is distorted and altered, first of all civilization itself. One by one all the voices are silenced.

Those few that may still be heard speak only to deny their own past. No use in resuscitating them. We do not believe in that kind of miracle: and all the efforts of the saviours of peoples in decline are not worth as much as a tiny spark of energy growing within another race that is rising.[10]

Everywhere photography became part of the commercial, cultural, and religious penetration of the West, thus assuming a hybrid role. On the one hand, it attempted to record a world, that of non-European cultures, at the very moment it came into contact with nineteenth-century ideas of progress; on the other hand, it faithfully mirrored the dreams, aspirations, and illusions of contemporary society. Around the middle of the century these aspirations were crystallizing into two opposite ideals: The first, as we have seen, defended a Europe entrusted with an impelling mission to cultivate and civilize the barbarous regions that composed the rest of the world; the second contrasted a gray Europe, disfigured by the Industrial Revolution and unable to offer any more space to individual initiative, with a somewhat ungeographical and largely imaginary East. So often antithetical urges and reactions coexist in the work of the artist. The celebration of a greater Europe exporting her dynamism and enthusiasm to a continent "forgotten by the flame of civilization" was counterbalanced by deeper sentiments toward a nature and a world yet untamed. The perception of a savage, unsullied grandeur mingled with anticipations of the ruthless and relentless march of "progress."

Undoubtedly, the photographers' primary role as witnesses was, more than in any other art, to document man's progress into the unexplored regions of the continent. While sensationalism and exalted rhetoric played their parts in painting, photography recorded with less formal presumption and greater sincerity the fearful changes, almost magical in their devasting consequences, that marked the decline of the traditional African world.

From Cape to Cairo—A Walk Across Africa

On June 9, 1788, at St. Albans Tavern in Pall Mall in London, nine men sat around a table enjoying some good beef and old port. All were upper-class and wealthy and shared the same enlightened interests. They were members of the Saturday's Club, a small association of twelve people. Among the nine present that evening were Sir Joseph Banks, botanist and president of the Royal Society, as well as secretary to the Dilettanti Society (interested in archaeology); the abolitionist Earl of Galloway; the Quaker Henry Beaufoy; the Bishop of Llandaff, professor of chemistry at Oxford; and Sir John Sinclair, pioneer in the field of statistics and future governor of India. Some indication of what they said and discussed may be gleaned from what Beaufoy wrote later:

While we continue ignorant of so large a portion of the globe, that ignorance must be considered as a degree of reproach on the present age. Sensible of this stigma, and desirous of rescuing the age from a charge of ignorance, which, in other respects, belongs so little to its character, a few individuals, strongly impressed with a conviction of the practicability and utility of thus enlarging the fund of human knowledge, have formed the Plan of an Association promoting the Discovery of the Interior parts of Africa. . . . The map of the interior regions of Africa is still a great white spot on which the geographer . . . has traced out with an uncertain hand a few names of unexplored rivers and doubtful names.[11]

The enigma of the River Niger was the first to be solved. It had been mentioned even by Ptolemy, and later by Arab geographers, who had called it "the Nile of the Negroes." But the European world knew neither its sources nor its mouths, nor even in which direction it flowed.

The founders of the African Association lost no time. Within four days after their dinner they had found two desperate explorers: John Ledyard, an American soldier of fortune, and Simon Lucas, a former wine merchant who had been a prisoner of the Moors and British vice-consul in Morocco. Ledyard was to cross Africa from east to west starting from Cairo, and Lucas from north to south starting from Tripoli. Both were badly prepared and insufficiently equipped, with no maps, scant supplies, and little money—Banks, who was treasurer, and Beaufoy were persuaded that in such an undertaking poverty was better protection than wealth. With a hundred pounds sterling between them, the two men did not get far. The American died of an unknown illness shortly after leaving Cairo, while Lucas, though disguised as a Turk, was forced to return to Tripoli, having been driven back by warrior tribes of the Fezzan.

No better luck was reserved for the Association's third explorer, the retired major Daniel Houghton, who left the mouth of the Gambia River and went north in search of Timbuktu; his remains were found years later in a village called Simbing (in today's Mali) about 160 miles north of the Niger and perhaps 500 miles short of Timbuktu. But he had penetrated the interior of the country farther than any other European had yet done.

The fourth explorer engaged by the African Association was Mungo Park, a Scottish physician with a passion for travel. Starting from the mouth of the Gambia River, he moved north along the route previously traced by Houghton, penetrating into the forbidden depths of the continent. His journey lasted thirteen months, and he returned home after endless adventures, having reached the Niger on June 20, 1796.

In geographical terms, Mungo Park had only scratched the surface of Africa; the enigma of the Niger remained unsolved, and Timbuktu was still far away.

But—as one would say today—he had created a new image of the adventurous, romantic, solitary, courageous explorer, able to cope with any kind of danger. The book Park wrote about his adventure became an immediate best seller and in effect founded a new literary genre destined to captivate the imaginations of generations of readers.

Six years later Park, grown weary of family life and of practicing medicine in Scotland, returned to Africa for his second expedition. This time he was not alone: accompanying him were his brother-in-law, a friend, and thirty-six convicts who had been promised freedom at the expedition's conclusion. There was also one Negro, the Mandinga guide Isaaco. On August 9, Park reached the Niger at Segou after having lost three-quarters of his men either to disease or to brigands. He sent Isaaco back with two letters, one for his wife and one for Banks, and that was his last sign of life. Isaaco returned to Sagou a few years later and reported that Mungo Park had died in an ambush at a place called Boussa Rapids.

The enigma of the Niger was, however, solved only twenty-five years later by the Lander brothers, who succeeded in descending the river from Boussa to the ocean. But the Niger was not the only destination in this part of Africa to attract explorers. There remained also the semi-mythical city of Timbuktu.

Tombuto is situated within twelve miles of a certaine branch of Niger. . . . there is a most stately temple to be seene, the wals thereof are made of stone and lime, and a princely palace also built by a most excellent workman. . . . Here are many shops of artificers and merchants and especially of such as weave linen and cotton cloth. . . . The inhabitants, and especially strangers are exceeding rich. . . . The rich king of Tombuto hath many plates and scepters of gold, some whereof weigh 1,300 pounds; and he keeps a magnificent and well-furbished court. . . . He hath alwaies 3,000 horsemen, and a great number of footmen that shoot poysoned arrowes, attending upon him. . . . Here are great stores of doctors, judges, priests and other learned men, that are bountifully maintained at the kings cost and charges. And hither are brought diverse manuscripts or written bookes out of Barbarie, which are sold for more money than any other merchandize.[12]

So wrote Leo Africanus, the sixteenth-century Moor from Granada, and it was obvious that the name of Timbuktu had acquired a magic fascination.

In the 1820s, Clapperton, Denham, and Oudney attempted to reach Bornou from the north. The black empire of Bornou together with the Kanem stretched from Nigeria and Lake Chad as far north as the Tibesti and Fezzan. It had been founded by the Sefuwa dynasty, which probably had its origins in the Yemen or among Berber tribes of the Sahara. Although the empire was in theory subject to the laws of the Koran, it would appear from the prevalence of matriarchal practices and folkways that many indigenous characteristics of the black society were conserved. The Bornou empire fell into decline around the beginning of the nineteenth century, and after the Berlin Conference its whole territory was assigned to France. The first white man to reach Timbuktu was the Frenchman René Caillé, who returned to Europe with news of a hitherto completely unknown world: that of black Islamic populations hidden beyond the Saharan savannas. Also Denham described the solemn audiences granted by the mai, Bornou's absolute sovereign, and these spurred the curiosity and imagination of the larger public. From 1815 to 1856 the German pastor Heinrich Barth, linguist, historian, geographer, and naturalist, traveled the western Sudan and produced an exceptional documentation, which became the essential source of information on these territories for the following forty years.

The next European adventure in the exploration of Africa was the search for the sources of the Nile, the river along which one of the greatest of human civilizations had developed. For almost two thousand years white men had tried to go up the river, but all their efforts had been defeated: In 460 B.C. Herodotus got as far as the cataracts of the Nile at Aswan, and the Romans had tried but lost themselves in the papyrus swamps. In his famous "mappamundi" Ptolemy portrayed the Nile as originating from two large lakes, far south in the region of the snowcapped Mountains of the Moon. Then the Western world had lost interest, with the exception of the search for Prester John, undertaken by two Portuguese Jesuits, who reached Lake Tana, and a hundred and fifty years later the attempt made by the Scottish explorer James Bruce, who followed the route established by the two Jesuits. In French history, Napoleon's expedition to Egypt represents a military failure marked by the disaster of Abukir of August 1, 1795, but for Egypt it meant the beginning of its modern cultural and political history. The competition between Britain and France for the control of the Red Sea and later the opening of the Suez Canal became a major incentive for the discovery of the sources of the Nile.

It is at this juncture that the history of geographical exploration merges into that of religious mission. Those that came nearest to the solution were the German missionaries of the Church Missionary Society, Johann Ludwig Krapf, Johannes Rebmann, and Jakob Erhard, who discovered Kilimanjaro and Mount Kenya.

In 1856 Britain's Geographical Society absorbed the African Association and promoted the first expedition of Sir Richard Francis Burton to discover the sources of the Nile. At that time Burton was thirty-six years old and had a great deal of colonial experience behind him. After having studied in France and Italy and at Oxford, he had spent seven years in a rather unorthodox and anomalous military career in India, where he used to disguise himself as a native merchant to spy in the bazaars. As an officer he was hot-tempered and intolerant of military discipline. But he was also a very courageous man, and he mastered a great number of languages and dialects. He translated *The Thousand and One Nights* together with a number of other Oriental love stories, and this gave him a reputation for libertinism. He seemed possessed of two quite different and contrasting natures: a methodical scholar and a romantic poet; a fussy hypochondriac and a libertine; an intellectual and a man of action. Burton had already traveled to Mecca disguised as an Afghan physician, and had undertaken just as dangerous an expedition to the forbidden city of Harrar. On that occasion he was accompanied by John Hanning Speke, whom he also chose as companion in the expedition to the sources of the Nile.

Speke, six years younger than Burton, had also done military service in India and had fought in the Punjab. He was a man who prepared his plans with great care, working out precise objectives, and once having made a decision, would proceed with great caution and resolution. But he lacked a sense of humor or a natural disposition to make friends. Speke was completely different in character from Burton, who, by choosing him, had thought to gain a follower and instead found a rival. Burton had made the first of a series of mistakes that were to afflict his life.

The two arrived in Zanzibar in December 1856 and, after a few months spent preparing for the expedition and then a visit to the old missionary Rebmann in June 1857, they arrived at Bogomayo in present-day Tanzania. "Bogomayo" means "lift the load from your heart." It was the starting point of the Arab caravans journeying into the interior. The caravans followed roads that had never been traced on maps, but they proceeded safely from village to village and from one trading post to the other. After a year or two the merchants would return to the coast with their loads of ivory, gold, and slaves.

The journey of Burton and Speke presented no overwhelming difficulties, but proceeded very slowly because of disease, the continual desertion of native carriers, and the toll payments demanded by every tribal chieftain. After reaching Tabora, then the most important Arab commercial station, the two men thought it wise to have a period of rest and to gather some geographical information on the region.

"There was an astonishing contrast," Burton wrote, "between the open hospitality and friendliness of this really noble race [the Arabs] and the meanness and egotism of the African savage: a heart of flesh and blood against a heart of stone."[13] He found himself with people of his own kind, grave and courteous men with beards and turbans and clad in long white tunics. That they were slave-traders did not disturb him.

Tabora is almost equidistant from Lake Tanganyika to the west and Lake Victoria to the north. As head of the expedition Burton had to make his decision, and here he made his second mistake: He chose to go west in the direction of Lake Tanganyika. Thus the two explorers were the first Europeans to set eyes on the great lake that might have been the source of the Nile but was not. The outflowing River Rusizi flows south, while the lake is only 770 meters above sea level—too low for giving birth to the Nile.

Burton was heartbroken. He and Speke returned to Tabora, both of them now ill—Burton with ulcers of the mouth and Speke with ophthalmia. Here Burton made another mistake: He decided to remain in Tabora to reorganize the caravan and to complete his travel notes. Speke, however, was anxious to search for Lake Nyasa, which the Arabs had described as being even larger than Lake Tanganyika. He therefore traveled north, with Burton quite content to let him go. Speke proceeded with forced marches until, at the beginning of August, he reached the lake that was later given the name of Victoria.

With astonishing certainty Speke declared he had found the source of the Nile. "I no longer felt any doubt," he wrote, "that the lake at my feet gave birth to that interesting river, whose source has been the subject of so much speculation and the object of so many explorers."[14] He was of course right, but had no way of proving it: All he had in fact seen for three days was an immense sheet of water, but he had not discovered any effluent going north. He could not even tell whether he had found a single lake or two or even more lakes.

Speke returned to Tabora, where the simmering tension between him and Burton now erupted into misunderstandings and quarrels. Burton was not intransigent regarding Speke's claims; he only wanted to make clear that the latter had no solid ground whatever on which to base his hasty assertions, which, so far, could only be considered suppositions. The two men returned to the coast broken by fever and no longer speaking to each other. Speke went on immediately to England, while Burton remained in Aden for a rest.

Without interference from Burton, Speke managed to obtain from the Royal Geographical Society sponsorship for a second expedition to Africa. In 1860, together with a new companion, James Augustus Grant, another former officer of the Indian army, Speke took the same road to Tabora and from there to Lake Victoria, where he found the northern effluent. Speke and Grant had already been in Africa for two years when they started their journey to the north trying to follow the course of the river which they thought to be the Nile.

On February 13, 1863, Speke and Grant reached Gondokoro. They saw a red brick building and the shed of the Austrian Mission. Speke wrote, "A man came running toward us . . . speaking English. . . . My old friend Baker, who in Ceylon had been known for his sportive exploits, came to shake my hand."[15]

Samuel Baker, the son of a wealthy landowner, had studied in Germany; he had a passion for traveling and big-game hunting, and had shot elephants in Ceylon, tigers in India, and bears in the Balkans. In 1860 he had left his three children from his first marriage with English relatives and departed for Africa accompanied by his second wife, a beautiful Hungarian lady, born Florence Niniam von Sass, fifteen years younger than he. Baker's intention was to navigate the Nile up to the Sudan and to learn Arabic during the journey. He carried supplies of delicious food from Fortnum & Mason's, as well as guns he had designed himself. His equipment had been bought in the best shops in London.

One year after leaving Cairo he arrived at Khartoum, where he received an assignment from the Royal Geographical Society to search for Speke and Grant. This assignment together with one thousand pounds sterling had previously been given to John Petherick, British vice-consul in Khartoum, who had traveled south together with his wife, but of whom no news had been received for several months. Baker went up the Nile and after a journey that lasted one year and covered a thousand miles, arrived at Gondokoro. Two weeks after his arrival Gondokoro was reached almost simultaneously by Speke and Grant as well as by the Pethericks. While Speke and Grant returned to Cairo, Baker decided to continue his journey up the Nile. He later wrote that he considered

. . . my mission as terminated, but . . . Speke and Grant with characteristic candour and generosity gave me a map of their route, showing that they had been unable to complete the actual exploration of the Nile, and that a most important portion remained to be demonstrated. . . .[16]

A year later Baker and his wife reached Lake Luta Nizige, which he named Lake Albert. Here is his description of the event: "I rushed into the lake, and thirsty with heat and fatigue, with a heart full of gratitude, I drank deeply from the Source of the Nile."[17]

Thus, to the already existing problems of Nile exploration another was added.

In September 1864, the British Association for the Advancement of Science held a meeting in Bath to discuss the controversial aspects of what the popular press had called the "Nile Duel." But one day before a debate between the two great rivals Burton and Speke was to take place, Speke was killed in a tragic accident during a hunting party on his uncle's estate. Some said he had committed suicide, out of dread of this face-to-face confrontation with Burton, a rumor that persisted for several years.

Sir Richard Murchison, at that time president of the Royal Geographical Society, thought that the best way to solve the controversy over the sources of the Nile was to send someone to ascertain the truth on the spot. His choice fell on the missionary Dr. David Livingstone, the foremost expert on African missions. Livingstone was fifty-two years old and had twenty-five years experience of Africa. After having finished his medical studies, he had asked to be sent to Kuruman, a missionary station 600 miles north of the Orange River.

In those times a missionary was supposed to remain all his life in the place he had chosen, and to concentrate on the religious conversion of the surrounding population. But a month after his arrival, Livingstone was already planning to travel north and explore regions never yet visited by a white man. In Kuruman, he married the daughter of the missionary Robert Moffat, Mary, who would bear him five children. During the ten years between 1846 and 1856, he first explored the upper and lower basins of the Zambezi River and crossed Central Africa from Luanda (Angola) to Quelimane (Mozambique). During this third journey (1858–64) he discovered Lake Nyasa, where he founded a missionary station that was to become the nucleus of the future British colony of Nyasaland.

In a letter to Professor Sedgwich, a short time before starting his Zambezi expedition, Livingstone wrote:

To give you a clear idea of my objectives I may say that they contain more than what they are apparently aiming at. They are not aimed at exploration alone. I am, in fact, leaving with the intention to bring benefit to the natives as well as to my compatriots. I am taking with me a professional geologist who should indicate the mineral resources of the country, a botanist to prepare a complete report on the possibilities of agricultural production, an artist to illustrate the landscapes, a naval officer to check the possibilities of river navigation and a moral agent who should give a Christian basis to anything that may be founded. The immediate aim of this whole organisation consists in the development of the African trade and the promotion of civilization.

But what I dare not tell anybody else but you, to whom I have complete trust, is that the outcome of this expedition may lead to the establishment of a British colony within the rich highlands of Central Africa.[18]

In 1864 Livingstone returned to England, where he had achieved immense popularity and his books had become best sellers. The entire world was moved to pity for the plight of the unfortunate Negroes, victims of the Arab slave traders, and everybody was enthusiastic about the evangelical work of the "good doctor" among the heathen. Murchison's choice was therefore more than justi-

fied, and so in 1866 Livingstone left for his last journey to the Dark Continent. No expedition had ever been based on as many wrong suppositions as was this one: It was supposed to search for the origins of a river in a region where there were no rivers, it was supposed to be an expedition against slavery without the means to fight slavery, it was supposed to be the journey of one solitary man who thought he could achieve the impossible, that is, to cross Africa without arms and assistance.

For almost two years nothing more was heard from Livingstone. However, after a series of incredible wanderings he was saved by Arab slave drivers—that is, by men whose trade he had been expected to oppose. Eventually he was found by Henry M. Stanley, when the latter reached Ujiji on November 10, 1871. Livingstone described his circumstances at the moment of meeting:

When my spirits had fallen into utter depression, the good Samarithan was already very near. One morning Suzy came running toward me and breathlessly announced: 'An Englishman! I saw him!' and she darted away to meet him. The American flag at the head of the caravan showed the stranger's nationality. When I saw the bales of supplies, the tin washbasins, the pots and large pans and all the rest, I thought: "There's a traveller who has at his disposal all facilities, not a poor devil like myself."[19]

Stanley's finding of Livingstone was what he became famous for above all else. But his later enterprises were really far more important. In his book *The White Nile,* Alan Moorehead defines him as a new type of man in Africa: the businessman-explorer. Stanley did not go to Africa to propagate the word of God or to abolish slavery, nor did he show any real interest in botany, anthropology, or geology. He went simply to make a name for himself.

In an expedition of 1876–77, sponsored by the London *Daily Telegraph* and the New York *Herald Tribune,* Stanley descended the Loualaba River as far as the Atlantic coast, thereby showing that this waterway was in fact the upper course of the Congo River. He had thus resolved the last of the problems that for eighty years had been matters of such intense dispute among explorers. When he emerged from the jungle and appeared on the Atlantic coast, after suffering incredible hardships and losing two-thirds of his companions, his newspapers were able to publish the story of one of the greatest adventures of the century.

Two years later, however, he returned to Africa under different conditions. He traveled under a false name and made repeated moves to deflect the attention of potential spies. The few who did know he was in Africa could only suspect that he had "some commercial project" in mind. The truth was that Stanley was now being financed by King Leopold II of Belgium, who wanted "personally" to purchase a slice of the continent. Leopold had written to Stanley: "There is no question of Belgian colonies, but to create a new state, as large as possible, and to run it. . . . the king, as a private citizen, wants to possess some properties in Africa. Belgium needs neither a colony nor territories. Mr. Stanley should therefore purchase lands or obtain them as concessions."[20]

This incredible project was realized, and France, feeling that it had to protect its own interests, hurriedly organized a second expedition, led by a Frenchman of Italian origins, Savorgnan de Brazza, who in previous years had explored Gabon and the Congo-Brazzaville. When the two explorers met at Stanley Pool in 1881, France could thus claim its own sovereign rights over the territories on the right side of the Congo River. The exploration of Africa was now exclusively dominated by commercial interests.

2

THE
LONG INTERLUDE

EXPANSION AND
COLONIZATION

Strange dawn. The morning of Occident in black Africa was spangled over with smiles, with cannon shots, with shining glass beads. . . . It was a morning of accouchement: the known world was enriching itself by a birth that took place in mire and blood.
—CHEIKH HAMIDOU KANE, *Ambiguous Adventure*

On February 23, 1885, in Berlin, four days before the official closing date, the delegates of fourteen European nations proclaimed in the General Act of the Conference the recognition of freedom of trade in all Central Africa, from one ocean to the other, and the official adoption of the German doctrine of the "hinterland." According to this doctrine every nation with possessions along the African coast had the right not only to dispose of the territory immediately behind them, but also to enlarge its borders to its own liking, as long as this did not harm the interests of a neighboring European colony. The Berlin Conference ratified once and for all the "great diplomatic game" of the division of Africa. The years that followed witnessed an incredible rush to gain territories, with everywhere the establishment of administrative bases in order to prove the "effective occupation" of those lands that in the past had been acquired through the "native negotiations" of the explorers or by inter-European diplomatic agreements. This period of expansion coincides with the suffocation of the last movements of native resistance, until the Europeans remained sole masters of the field. At the end of the century the political geography of the continent looked totally different from what it had been twenty years earlier: By 1902, in the whole continent, only three independent countries—Morocco, Liberia, and Ethiopia—were left; the rest was divided among the colonial possessions of England, France, Belgium, Germany, Portugal, Italy, Spain, and Turkcy. Thc gcopolitical map of Africa stayed fixed at the time of decolonization, and even though the colors by which the various states are indicated have changed, the borderlines have remained largely the same.

The public announcement of the invention of photography coincided with landmarks of military conquest and colonial settlement, which heralded an era of unparalleled expansion and consolidation uniquely documented in photographs. The Zulu Wars and a group of tourists in Egypt, gold-mining operations in South Africa and a missionary school in Rhodesia, the opening of the Suez Canal and archaeological excavations in Tunisia: As photography spread overseas, these were the sort of events the photographer would attempt to record.

What would one not give to have photographs of the Pharaohs or the Caesars, of the travellers, and their observations, who supplied Ptolemy with his early record of the world, of Marco Polo, and the places and peoples he visited on his arduous journey? We are now making history, and the sun picture supplies the means of passing down a record of what we are, and what we have achieved in this nineteenth century of our progress.

This expression of faith in the importance of photography was made by John Thomson in a talk on exploration and photography delivered to the geographical section of the British Association in Cardiff, Wales, on April 24, 1891. Thus the photographic lens followed the coming of the white man, who imposed his steel, his religion, his brains, his will, on a great continent and its inhabitants, and the slow metamorphosis of the European from explorer and merchant to conqueror and exploiter, from ordinary buyer to master.

At first, African colonization was inspired by powerful private companies that assumed political responsibility often long before the state officially intervened. These companies simply took on sovereign power over enormous regions, securing them with their own diplomacy and administering them directly according to laws they themselves wrote, while their own private police forces made sure they were obeyed. This strange situation was partly the consequence of the rapidity with which the Industrial Revolution developed in Europe. The urgent need for new commercial outlets and cheap raw materials forced European capitalism to search for as yet unexploited territories and possibly to administer them without intermediaries or control. Only later did strategic and political considerations force governments to step in, and the companies' protectorates were transformed into colonies.

The colonies were generally a mercantile creation, however, essentially like a formidable organization of international exchange. This was particularly true of the British empire, and to a lesser degree the French one, which was more like an intensely bureaucratized military conquest, whereas the Spanish colonies were a kind of feudal appanage run by the Church. The colonial empires were created by navigators, corsairs, shipbuilders, pioneers, farmers, businessmen, bankers, technicians, all in search of fortune, all people who, once the stage of violence was past, wherever they arrived, were able to construct around them fertile cooperative interests, productive activities, alliances, support. They were champions of the idea that the best reason for crossing the seas, the mountains, and the deserts was to buy and sell. In time the rhythm of production was gradually intensified in order to meet the home country's growing demand, usually to the disadvantage of the local laborers.

In 1902 young Winston Churchill wrote:

What enterprise that an enlightened community may attempt is more noble and more profitable than the reclamation from barbarism of fertile regions and large populations? To give peace to warring tribes, to administer justice where all was violence, to strike the chains off the slave, to draw the richness from the soil, to plant the earliest seeds of commercial learning, to increase in whole peoples their capacities for pleasure and diminish their chances of pain—what more beautiful ideal or more valuable reward can inspire human effort? The act is virtuous, the exercise invigorating, and the result often extremely profitable. Yet as the mind turns from the wonderful cloudland of aspiration to the ugly scaffolding of attempt and achievement, a succession of opposite ideas arise. Industrious races are displayed stinted and starved for the sake of an expensive Imperialism which they can only enjoy, if they are well fed. Wild peoples, ignorant of their barbarism, callous of suffering, careless of life but tenacious of liberty, are seen to resist with fury the philanthropic invaders, and to perish in thousands before they are convinced of their mistake. The inevitable gap between conquest and dominion becomes filled with the figures of the greedy trader, the inopportune missionary, the ambitious soldier, and the lying speculator, who disquiet the minds of the conquered and excite the sordid appetites of the conquerors. And as the eye of thought rests on these sinister features, it hardly seems possible for us to believe that any fair prospect is approached by so foul a path.[1]

Such doubts were soon overthrown by the more "progressive" financiers and politicians endowed with more flair than moral restraint. Among the fiercest supporters of colonial exploitation were the French president Jules Ferry and Leopold II, king of the Belgians.

Colonization constituted a unique national experience for the European powers. It was at once a global idea and a concrete device: Not only did it impose on the world a certain concept of reality, but it also contained the means whereby that concept could be put immediately into practice. The true result of this process, which expanded in the period from the "mission of civilization" to decolonization, was to export the European state-machine outside the metropolitan territory. A small number of nations experimented on a planetary scale with the possibilities of modern technology, of titanic endeavor, and of economic power, with the professed aim of changing the world.

With the Treaty of Berlin in 1885, the European powers established the rules for the partition of the continent. Only 75 years later, the colonial era was in good part over. How durable was the influence of this comparatively short period on the traditional African (and European) way of life is still a matter of discussion, and even though it seems to have had a lesser impact than was for some time supposed, certain religious, cultural, political, and social changes did have a wide and decisive influence. The rapid development of the Industrial Revolution, the rise of the larger and richer middle class, and the creation of immense colonial empires gave Europe an overwhelming and intoxicating belief in its own moral and cultural superiority. And indeed, the sacred ideals of the bourgeoisie became the standards by which to judge the developmental stage of each non-Western people. Devotion to a relatively recent monotheistic religion allied with rigid Victorian morals, an unshakable belief in private property and material wealth, and academic art were what distinguished European "civilization" from the surrounding "savagery" and "barbarism." (Two world wars with their related atrocities and a number of unanticipated economic crises have, to be sure, significantly undermined this conviction of European superiority.)

In Africa, then, two radically different ways of experiencing reality, society, authority, and myth met in a titanic clash, sometimes succeeding in amalgamating: the European, open and distinguished by ideologies in rapid evolution; the African, cut off from the rest of the world and dominated by religion, tradition, and magic. The former, at the height of its power and continuously projected toward the "edge of outer darkness," eager for explorations and conquests; the latter confined in a small part of the world, prisoner of deep-rooted beliefs and of its own refusal to accept change.

The ten years before the Great War witnessed the passage from an initial phase of "demographic colonialism" to a capitalistic development that was never able to take off in full. The century was still young and the situation was already ripe for crisis. An English under-secretary wrote in one of his reports: "It is difficult to believe that in such a new centre so many controversies and conflicts of interest can develop. . . . The white man against the negro, the Indian against both . . . the officer against the civilian, the man from the coast against the one from the highlands . . . all these points of view, risen spontaneously, adopted honestly, sustained tenaciously, but not coordinated in one harmonious and general conception."[2]

The era ended with the First World War, when the dividing up of the continent was already concluded and an administrative organization typical of colonialism was firmly in place. Colonization has often been justified in terms of its material achievements on the continent, but the humanitarian component really never represented the main incentive. European culture was imposed on limited social sectors, often only in the interest of the colonizer and without any consideration for the life aspirations of the African societies or their harmonious cultural development. The vast transportation network, the development of a modern agriculture and embryonic industries, health care and construction of hospitals benefited only a small number of Africans. Public education, although very developed in some colonies, was confined to lower grades and to the formation of cheap auxiliary cadres for the large European financial groups established in Africa and for the colonial bureaucracy. The widely publicized fight against tropical diseases went into effect only when epidemics threatened the supply of native labor. In the whole continent, decolonization was accompanied by hard and tormented battles and hopes that in most cases were shattered.

N.D. Phot. (French)
The Ruins of Timgad. View of the Decumanus Maximus
gelatin silver print
Algeria, ca. 1900
Coll. Fondazione Sella e Istituto di Fotografia Alpina "Vittorio Sella"

The African, dwarfed by nature or the majestic remains of ancient cultures, unconsciously inhabited the trappings of eighteenth-century notions of the picturesque and sublime. His figure is often designed to be at one with nature, engulfed in space, hinting at some ideal and hidden harmony.

VITTORIO SELLA (Italian, 1859–1943)
Mt. Ruwenzori from a Hill on the Road Between Butiti and Fort Portal
gelatin silver print
Uganda, 1906
Coll. Fondazione Sella e Istituto di Fotografia Alpina "Vittorio Sella"

"May 28. We leave at half past five and after little more than an hour's walk we are delighted to see for the first time the Ruwenzori . . . a wonderful landscape. Rolling hills with the dark green spots of the euphorbias, light, jagged with acacias; here and there reddish or brown yellow fields form the foreground and at a greater distance become more confused in the gauzy atmosphere of the mighty buttresses of this range filled with mystery. The solemnity of the dark and stormy sky makes the sight even more stirring . . ."

—*From Vittorio Sella's travel diary*

GIOVANNI DE SIMONI (Italian)
Restoration of Abu-Simbel
Egypt, ca. 1910
Coll. Monas Hierogliphica, Milan

30

ABDULLAH BROTHERS
The Sphinx of Ghizeh
albumen
Egypt, ca. 1890
Private Coll.

Flaubert to his mother, from Cairo, December 14, 1849: "We arrived at the foot of the hill where the Pyramids stand eight days ago at four in the evening. I couldn't resist, I set my horse off at full gallop. Maxime followed me and I arrived at the foot of the Sphinx. . . . I suddenly felt dizzy, and my companion was white as the paper I am using to write you. At the sunset the Sphinx and the three pyramids, now all pink, seemed drowned in the light; the old monster looked at us with a terrifying and still expression."

—*Flaubert, Correspondence,* vol. I, pp. 346–7

(Photographer Unknown)
Group of Warriors
East Africa, ca. 1880
Coll. Civici Musei, Pavia

LOANDA

J.A.CE MORAES

J. A. DA CUNHA MORAES (Portuguese)
Gentleman farmer and boy
albumen on carte-de-visite
Mossamedes, Angola, ca. 1870
Coll. Monas Hierogliphica, Milan

35

(Photographer Unknown)
Tourists climbing the Great Pyramid
albumen
Egypt, ca. 1890
Private Coll.

Forty years before this photograph was taken, Flaubert had written, "It's very ravaged and damaged, not by the course of time, but by tourists and scholars."

(Photographer Unknown)
Chief Regulo Moquepera, his two sons and some of his wives
Portuguese Africa, ca. 1900
Coll. Monas Hierogliphica, Milan

The idyllic and nostalgic vision Romantics had of the Africans was often in open contrast with the judgments expressed by the early travelers. The great explorer Burton regarded the Africans' religion as nothing but "vague nameless fear," lacking in any moral code: "Marriage, which for Christians is of the utmost importance and for Muslims much less, is an event that means little to them and happens with great frequency. Polygamy is unlimited and the chiefs are proud of the number of their wives, which varies from twelve to three hundred."

J. A. DA CUNHA MORAES (Portuguese)
Banana, on the Banks of the River Zaire
albumen
Angola, ca. 1880
Coll. Monas Hierogliphica, Milan

"Sometimes we came upon a station close by the bank, clinging the skirts of the unknown, and the white men rushing out of a tumbledown hovel, with great gestures of joy and surprise and welcome, seemed very strange—had the appearance of being held there captive by a spell. The word ivory would ring in the air for a while—and on we went again in the silence, along empty reaches, round still bends, between high walls of our winding way, reverberating in hollow claps the ponderous beat of the stern wheel." Joseph Conrad, *Heart of Darkness*.

(Photographer Unknown)
Tractor, Boaventoranca Farm
albumen
Novo Redondo, Portuguese Africa, ca. 1880
Coll. Monas Hierogliphica

The devastating action of progress left continually deeper marks
on the natural environment. The artificial landscape it created, and
the wounds and ravages it inflicted upon the soil, went hand in
hand with the exploitation of the native people.

(Photographer Unknown)
Muslim praying
gelatin silver print
Somalia or Eritrea, ca. 1910

44   Archivio Provinciale dei Padri Cappuccini, Milan

J. A. DA CUNHA MORAES
  (Portuguese)
African Lady
albumen
Loanda, Angola, ca. 1870
Coll. Monas Hierogliphica, Milan

Right
LEHNERT & LANDROCK (German)
Tunis. Rue Sidi ben Arous
photogravure
from the book *Picturesque North Africa*
Tunisia, ca. 1900
Coll. Monas Hierogliphica, Milan

Africa meant a journey further and further
backward in time as the traveler proceeded toward the heart of the continent. From the moment he landed, even in those countries on the
coast where European influence was most felt,
life seemed to amble along in ancient ways and
rhythms, forgotten in Europe many centuries
ago, to such a degree that Flaubert exclaimed:
"Here is the Orient of the Middle Ages, of the
Mameluks, of the Barbarians."

LEHNERT AND LANDROCK (German)
Native Scenery During the Inundation
albumen
Egypt, ca. 1900
Coll. Monas Hierogliphica, Milan

48

(Photographer Unknown)
Boer War, Lieutenant Col. W. P. Pulteney and his troops crossing Buffalo
River, Sept. 1901
Coll. Monas Hierogliphica, Milan

The Boer War might just have been one more of the countless wars of conquest the British fought in Africa, except for the fact that this time the enemies were not "natives," but white settlers of Dutch and German descent. After four years of stubborn guerrilla warfare, the Boers surrendered their independence in 1902. The consequences of this war for Africa were profound. Besides show-ing a dramatic breach in white unity in Africa, it represented a major lost opportunity to bring about peaceful political change among nonwhites in South Africa. In an attempt at conciliation, the British bestowed on the Boers the right to decide whether or not the vote should be given to blacks. Faithful to their white supremacist traditions, the Boers decided in the negative.

LUCA COMERIO (Italian, 1878–1940)
Artillery mounted on camels
Libya, 1911
Coll. Monas Hierogliphica, Milan

As the European powers occupied African territories by force, the official iconography exalted the images of those who would become the pillars of the great colonial empires: the soldier, the civil servant, the settler. Among these, the soldier got the lion's share: the occupation of African land proceeded through an endless series of wars and massacres, which not only "broadened the European peoples' point of view" but offered opportunities for heroic performances and rich inspiration for celebrative art.

(Photographer Unknown)
Boer War: sentry duty at the English camp
Slingerfontein, South Africa, 1900
Private Coll.

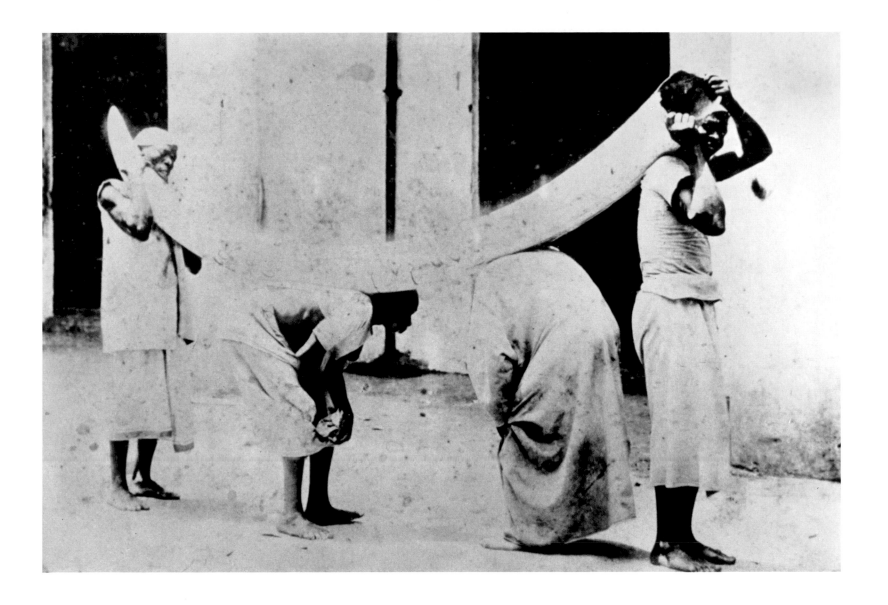

A. C. GOMES
Ivory tusk: Weighing 200 lbs.
albumen
East Africa, ca. 1880
Private Coll.

For centuries, white and black ivory represented the two most valuable African export commodities. The trade in both was controlled by the Arabs, who were the true pioneers in opening up the African interior. The abolition of the slave trade and the gradual European occupation of the African coasts ruined the Arab merchants, and little by little their operations were taken over by European traders. Even missionaries became involved—in the early 1860s, Livingstone reported: "I know of two of the Wesleyan Society who have turned renegade. One, a Mr. Archbell, is one of the greatest land speculators in Natal and has about 18,000 acres still in hand. He still has the impudence to go occasionally into the pulpit."

J. PASCAL SEBAH (Turkish)
Desert scene
albumen
Egypt, ca. 1870
Coll. Monas Hierogliphica, Milan

Left
(Photographer Unknown)
Arab ballad singer
albumen
Egypt, ca. 1880
Private Coll.

Photographers documented the most impressive features of the lands and the native populations of the new European colonial possessions, though their work was obviously influenced by the need to produce a saleable product.

Right
(Photographer Unknown) (Italian)
Girl of Beggiuk tribe
photogravure
Eritrea, ca. 1900
Coll. Monas Hierogliphica, Milan

The relationship between the white man and the native woman was often perceived as that between colonizer and colonized country, in which exotic transgression is interpreted as a return to an immediacy of passion that the Western world had long repressed. In a very peculiar way eroticism became a medium for establishing contact, for penetrating the secrets of nature, the reality and the "otherness" of the continent. The seduction and conquest of the African woman became a metaphor for the conquest of Africa itself. A powerful erotic symbolism linked a woman's femininity so strongly to the attraction of the land that they became one single idea, and to both were attributed the same irresistible, deadly charm.

(Photographer Unknown)
Group of Danakils (Obock)
Somalia, ca. 1870

Left
LUIGI FIORILLO (Italian)
Observation balloon
Abyssinia, ca. 1895
Coll. Monas Hierogliphica, Milan

Right
LUIGI FIORILLO (Italian)
Luigi Robecchi-Bricchetti entombed in a sarcophagus
Egypt, ca. 1880
Coll. Civici Musei, Pavia

Exoticism in portraits expressed itself in Western culture through the choice of costumes and poses ascribed to the natives of faraway lands.

A. LEROUX (French)
Fête au Marabout de Sidi Zour Zour à Biskra
coated photogravure
Algeria, ca. 1900
Coll. Monas Hierogliphica, Milan

LUCA COMERIO (Italian, 1878–1940)
Drummer boys
Libya, 1912
Coll. Monas Hierogliphica, Milan

All the colonial powers had special troops trained in accordance
with the specific climatic and geopolitical conditions of each colony. Particularly numerous were the so-called "coloured" troops,
greatly praised for their high efficiency and low cost.

RUDOLPH PÖCH (Austria, 1870–1921)
Thomas, a Basuto Policeman,
*   Stationed in Chansenfeld*
gelatin silver print
Botswana, 1907
Coll. Museum für Völkerkunde, Vienna

3

THE
AFRICAN

The figurative schemes of nineteenth-century painting are evidenced in a vast output that may be described as "genre painting," and its equivalent in a large sector of European photography. In the Muslim countries of Mediterranean Africa, where the earliest photographic activity is concentrated, photographers apparently freed themselves from the conventions of contemporary painting with greater difficulty. The contrast between the elegance of an ancient mosque and a turbaned mullah, or between a lotus-shaped Nilotic column and a fierce dragoman artfully leaning on its top, is a theme inherited from painting, made famous at the end of the eighteenth century by the painter William Pars and repeated extensively throughout the nineteenth century by photographers. The small figure, ubiquitous in European, and particularly English, landscape painting is another recurring motif in nineteenth-century photographs of Africa. The scaling of human figures in relation to landscape took on a special meaning in the early years of African photography. Sometimes the characters that populate the landscape seem little more than spatial coordinates. Dwarfed by nature or the majestic remains of ancient cultures, the African bore the trappings of the previous century's notions of the picturesque and sublime. In landscape the native figure is often designed to be at one with nature, engulfed in space, performing no particular action or movement, as if almost absent, part of the general mood of stillness and absorption, hinting at some ideal and hidden harmony between man and nature.

Beyond North Africa, this theme develops with ever-increasing strength. South of the desert, south of the cultivated antiquity of Egypt and the white citadels of the Muslims, the footprints of civilization grow fainter until they finally disappear in the vast rainforests of equatorial Africa. There, where the silent energy of nature is forever at work, lay the unsettled territories that were the proper environment and breeding ground for the "noble savage" celebrated by Rousseau, Chateaubriand, and the Lake Poets, which, far from representing culture, symbolized nature in its inviolate state. He was, as Rousseau wrote, the last survivor of a distant time when the human race was *"meilleure, plus sage et plus heureuse dans sa constitution primitive."* The formal unity in the photograph between the human figure and the natural surroundings implies a philosophical unity: To the cultivated explorer the dark inhabitant of the jungles appeared to be as much a part of Mother Nature as trees and rocks. Therefore the noble savage is the only figure that can be introduced in the artwork without disrupting the landscape, interpreted as a divine creation. The first Western travelers had not the vaguest idea of the great complexity of "primitive man." Of the savage they noticed his rejection of the conventions of European society, his physical beauty, his lustful innocence, all characteristics that helped to complete, beside the geographic discoveries, the real and imaginary map of the world. Such works as Rousseau's *Emile,* Bougainville's *Voyage autour du monde,* and Diderot's *Supplément au voyage de Bougainville* opened the way to the discovery of nature, of which the myth of the noble savage is a logical derivative. The entire eighteenth century is full of it. For such writers it was an active concept directed against the constrictions of feudal society, against the prejudices of contemporary morality, against everything that tried to deform man's free and natural spontaneity. For Rousseau the "natural man" corroborated the myth in a political context. The French Revolution proclaimed that all men are equal. On February 17, 1794, a black from Santo Domingo took the floor in the French Legislative Assembly and while the president and the deputies embraced him, Robespierre was heard to shout: "Citoyen Président, in the first row of the public gallery is sitting an old black woman. She is mad with joy. I invite you to order the secretaries to immortalize this fact in the protocol."

As time went by, however, the original concept changed: It ceased to be the idea of renewing society by giving it free and liberal foundations; instead the conviction took root that society was intrinsically and irremediably compromised, and that the only salvation lay in evasion and escape. In other words, from a myth "converging" toward a social reality it intended to reform, it changed into a "divergent" myth that placed itself outside this perverse reality which it rejected. The myth, which for some meant the pursuit of uncontaminated and innocent happiness, became for others picturesque exoticism, simple distraction, artistic fad. Mallarmé's poem ("I shall go away. Ship, with your swaying masts—lift your anchor towards exotic nature!") conveys the exact spirit of a prolific "official" artistic production that develops as the colonial empires continue to grow.

But still there remains the obstinate endeavor, shared by people of widely varying outlook, to overcome, in art and in life, man's growing alienation, resulting from the society that was rapidly denying its own revolutionary premises. Escape from Europe was seen as a tactic in the battle against the progressive impoverishment of spiritual and human values, an attempt to safeguard one's own integrity from the menace of a disheartening and unacceptable reality. Through the myths of the savage and primitivism, the artist was searching in the first place for himself, trying to free his deepest nature, stripping it of prejudices and conventions. "Civilization," wrote Paul Gauguin, "is gradually getting farther and farther away from me. I am beginning to think with simplicity, to have only little hatred towards my neighbour, actually to love him. I have all the joys of free life, both animal and human. I am escaping from fakery, I am entering into Nature."[1] The return to Nature in virgin lands overseas was the expression of a mystical longing for a paradise on earth uncontaminated by original sin, where it would be possible, by immersing oneself in nature, to be free of the prejudices of a hypocritical morality, to purify and redeem oneself, to become a "savage."

Delacroix explained the concept of the evolution of the sense of Beauty according to the romantic view:

We judge all the rest of the world from our narrow horizons: we do not throw off our petty habits, and our enthusiasm is often just as foolish as our indignation. We judge with the same arrogance works of art and those of nature. A person living in London or Paris may be farther away from having a proper sense of beauty than the illiterate inhabitant of a place where civilization has not yet arrived. We see beauty only through the imagination of poets and painters; the savage meets it at every step of his wandering life.

I am willing to admit that this man may have only a few moments to spare for poetical impressions, since we know very well that his main occupation is not to die of starvation. He must continuously fight a hostile environment to defend his wretched life. And yet the view of overwhelming sights and the force of a sort of primitive poetry can fill his heart with sentiments of admiration.[2]

The civilized man seemed an offense to nature, and as such a danger to the life of the savage, who is part of nature and obeys its laws; "he does not know any ambitions, nor does he lie to his neighbor or cheat him." As it was not possible to realize this radical change of life at home, many tried to carry out this transformation at the frontiers of Europe. According to Isak Dinesen, "Sometimes on a safari, or on the farm, in a moment of extreme tension, I have met the eyes of my native companions, and have felt that we were at a great distance from one another, and that they were wondering at my apprehension of our risk. It made me reflect that perhaps they were, in life itself, within their own element, such as we can never be, like fishes in deep water which for the life of them cannot understand our fear of drowning. This assurance, this art of swimming, they had, I thought, because they had preserved a knowledge that was lost by our first parents; Africa will teach it to you: that God and the Devil are one."[3] When this attempt clashed with reality and the changes produced by colonial expansion, and failed as well, no other way remained than to seek freedom in dreaming, in metaphysical evasion, or in one's innermost self.

But apart from the theoretical discussions and opinions of artists and philosophers, the difference between the concepts of the "noble savage" and of the "bad savage" was rather subtle. The fundamental analysis was the same and the sustainers of either concept agreed on one single version of the facts: The savage is a being governed by instincts alien to culture and civilization. On the other hand, their conclusions were diametrically opposed: For the former this state of nature was essentially a virtue, whereas for the latter it meant a vice based on brute force, which denied any moral and esthetic values and was therefore an evil that had to be fought. In the white man's opinion, the populations of inner Africa lived out a "monotonous," eventless history, "typical" of the Hamitic race. "To this Africa, everything that has happened in the history of the world is as if it had never taken place: its existence is still in the sun, which burns the blood and dries up any sentiment in the soul; its people, naked like the deserts and with a just as arid conscience, represent the cruelest beast of its fauna."[4]

The "beneficial violence" that obliterates boundaries, mixes races, "assimilating them, melting their characters and evolving them," never touched them. "Protected by the seas, by their forests, their endless deserts and vast moors, by the killing climate of their land, they had remained hidden and unknown for centuries."[5] According to many colonialists, not even the white man's iron and fire were able to shake them out of their atavistic indolence. Any civilizing action seemed bound to fail in its effort of elevating the black from his sad condition of immaturity and wildness. As a matter of fact, many believed that the blacks would share the destiny of the American Indians: Sooner or later they would disappear, overcome by progress, by their incapacity to evolve, which left them defenseless against the weapons, machines, and way of life of modern civilization. Some argued in religious terms that God, in denying the first inhabitants of the continent the capacity to become civilized, had destined them from the start to inevitable destruction. The true possessors of the continent were to be those who knew how to exploit its riches. In 1895, Cardinal Massaja wrote: "I was involved with a people who lived in purely wild conditions, who not only did not know what science was, but of whom one might not even expect that their minds could ever be applied to any concepts other than sensual ones."[6]

The famous Burton, although he was a scholar of the colored races and liked to travel in their countries, displayed a strange and contradictory contempt for the Africans, who in his opinion were to be blamed for the very fact of being wild and whom he considered all as "little delinquents with strong criminal tendencies." And he added: "They seem to belong to an infantile race which, without ever reaching the stage of maturity, detaches itself like a worn-out link from the great chain of intelligent nature." The Africans' religion was nothing but "vague nameless fear," and of course any moral code was lacking: "Marriage, which for Christians is of the utmost importance and for Muslims much less, is an event that means little to them and happens with great frequency. Polygamy is unlimited and the chiefs are proud of the number of their wives, which varies from twelve to three hundred."[7]

Another famous explorer, Samuel Baker, showed little sympathy for the natives: "As much as this horrible slavery system may be condemned, the results of emancipation have demonstrated that the negro does not love freedom, nor does he show the least gratitude to those who have broken his chains." Baker was convinced that the Africans were not and never would be similar to white men. He admitted only that during childhood the black "was superior, with a more lively intelligence than a white boy of the same age, but his mind does not develop any further; it promises fruits, but does not mature."

He also attacked the Africans for what he saw as the barbarousness and cruelty of their tribal customs. "A fascinating people, these poor negroes, as they are called by the English sympathizers," he exclaimed when a Nuego chief

showed the back and arms of his own wife covered with saw-toothed scars . . . he was very proud of having branded his wife like a wild animal. . . . Polygamy is a general custom; the number of wives depends exclusively on the man's wealth, just as happens in England with horses. In these regions there is nothing that resembles love . . . everything is essentially practical without any sentiment. Women are appreciated only because they are precious animals. . . . I am afraid this state of affairs will be a strong barrier against missionary work.[8]

At the end of the century, Mary Kingsley supplies more evidence on how the local populations were viewed at the time. It seems a curious opinion insofar as it is expressed by a woman, a lady considered emancipated, who thought she had discovered the reason why missionary evangelization in Africa had so often failed: The difference between the white man and the African was not a difference of degree but a difference of kind. The black man, in her view, was no more an underdeveloped white man than a rabbit was an underdeveloped hare. She thought that the mental differences between the two races were somewhat similar to those between the sexes among Europeans. "A great woman, either mentally or physically, will excel an ordinary man, but no woman ever equals a really great man. The missionary to the African has done what my father found them doing to the Polynesians, regarding the native minds as so many jugs only requiring to be emptied of the stuff which is in them and refilled with the particular form of dogma he is engaged in teaching, in order to make them equals to the white races."[9] The contact with Muslim North Africa was quite different: For many photographers it was an overwhelming experience, making them doubt whether what they saw and experienced was real. Drenched with Romantic motifs and literature, they found in Morocco's imperial cities, in Cairo, or in the surrounding deserts, the divine Orient of their dreams, pretending not to notice a reality already in full decadence, decrepit and corrupt. The Arab cities full of soldiers, merchants, prostitutes, cripples, suspect and splendid characters, offered countless subjects for their cameras. But more than anybody else, it was the Sultan who incarnated the height of Western fantasies, with his harems, the power of life and death over his subjects, his possession of both earthly and spiritual power as "defender of the faithful." "Everything around him spoke of his enormous power, the immense distance that separated him from all other men, a limitless submission, a fanatic devotion, a passion of fearful and wild love which seemed to ask to be proved by blood."[10]

Loti thus skillfully summarized the lasting impression (which in time would engender a whole series of not always positive commonplaces) produced by the impact with Islamic Africa. The Arabs appeared to be lost in a vague dream of eternity in which they lived without worrying about earthly tomorrows. They let the old walls crumble in the light of passing summers, the grass grow on the roofs, the carcasses of animals rot where they fell. "Their philosophy is simple: let's leave everything as it is and enjoy only the passing-by of the things that do not deceive, of beautiful creatures, beautiful horses, beautiful gardens and the scent of flowers."[11] But although from this civilization the germs of renewal seemed to have disappeared, it still remained the expression of a superb culture. The fact that some of its aspects were not understood did not diminish its fascination.

Quite different was the vision of the Central European photographer who seemed to find, in the immobility and the dignified gestures of the African, those lost gods which had been present throughout the century in German romanticism, from Heine to Nietzsche. German culture saw in the Africans men who, like those of classical antiquity, still embodied the forces of nature, the sense of the necessary and of the present. "If one thinks of the beautiful scenery that surrounded the ancient Greeks, how intimately close they could live to free nature, and how nearer to innocent nature was their sensitivity, their imagination, their habits and customs,"[12] then one could only envy the state in which the so-called primitive peoples, or, as Schiller called them, the "infantile" peoples, were living. In spite of the enormous distance that separated the civilized man's actions from the truths of nature, he felt he was ideally driven toward them, and the observation of primitive peoples with their surprising customs made it easier to compare and therefore realize his own lack of naturalness. The distinct classical echo of this call to reclaim a lost human dignity and balance was common, throughout the century, to the writings of personalities as different as Delacroix or De Amicis and bears witness to how thoroughly felt this theme was.

Fundamentally, everyone saw Africa and its inhabitants as his own culture made him see it. The English missionary Harry Johnston, who visited Uganda around 1890, remarked that the men in their long robes reminded him of the figures of saints: "They recalled the conventional pictures of evangelical piety, in which the blessed are walking in the valleys of Paradise."[13]

Lastly, there is a substantial body of ethnographic documentation guided by criteria of mere type classification according to the strictest rules of positivism, as well as by the urge to record faces and customs whose end seemed to be in sight. Among all the subjects photography dealt with all over the world, there is no doubt that some of the most beautiful works should be attributed to the broad category of ethnographical photography. Of course, there is also a large body of photographs that are not particularly exciting and some of dubious taste; in some portraits the African looks about as natural as an insect pinned on the entomologist's board, but this disappointing treatment can be ascribed more to the operator's mediocrity than to any veiled racism. These pictures are actually not much different from the ones turned out by thousands of small and large photographic studios in Europe and America with little technical skill and no artistic ambition. Portraits that showed picturesque and exotic costumes and customs of little-known and faraway populations assured the commercial photographer a prosperous market in Europe, and in their advertisements many photographic studios referred to the availability of collections of "native types" from which the tourist or the collector could make his choice. As new territories passed under the control of European administration, the enterprising photographer would document the most impressive features of the lands and populations of these new possessions.

The photographer of this kind of portrait had to face problems unknown to his colleague specializing in landscapes, particularly when the subjects were frightened of the camera. It was by no means uncommon for the camera, with its threatening cannon-like lens, to be at first mistaken for a weapon. Almost all operators who traveled to localities little visited by Westerners remarked on the unwillingness of their subjects to pose and the consequent unnaturalness of the resulting picture.

But little by little, things improved. As Samuel Bourne noted: "From the earliest days of the calotype, the curious tripod, with its mysterious chamber and mouth of brass, taught the natives that their conquerors were the inventors of other instruments beside the formidable guns of their artillery, which, though as suspicious perhaps in appearance, attained their object with less noise and smoke," and according to Gilbert Carter, who in 1893 was English governor in Lagos, at the close of the century those natives who had been more exposed to European ways began to appreciate photography's purpose: "I was much struck at the way they composed themselves to submit to this ordeal, and seemed to understand precisely what was required of them: I noticed the younger ones especially arranging their clothes, and even the old gray gave an additional touch to a kind of turban which she wore upon her head."[14]

The commercial photographers' work was obviously influenced by having to produce an attractive and saleable product; so often certain "typical" postures, clothes, and ornaments were the photographers' doing, for the sake of creating an effectual scene. In comparison, the production by many amateurs, colonial officials and scientists for the most part, although often inferior from a strictly technical point of view, gives a much more complete and accurate picture of the ethnic groups with whom these Europeans were, often for many years, in daily contact for work or study. Series of photographs grouped by racial types (placed against a checkered background for comparison with other races, and complete with anthropometrical measurements) were fairly typical, as were those showing the Africans in the exercise of their handicrafts and trades, their architecture, dress, and games.

European expansion drew the attention to populations that until then were little known or completely unknown and caused in a way increased scientific interest in the study of ethnology. The success of this new science (the Ethnological Society was founded in London in 1843), and its need for accurate representations of the human races, drove many photographers to document the topic. As can be expected the results were extremely varied: genre studies or tableaux that had little to do with reality beside portraits that responded to exact scientific criteria. Modern ethnology has taught us to see in the diversity of primitive cultures a rationality of its own, which has nothing to do with our scale of values; it has therefore taught us not to involve other cultures in our own projections, which, through the delusion of intuitive understanding, only annihilate the diversity.

In 1869 the British Colonial Office sent to the governors of the colonies a detailed circular letter asking them to collect and send to London photographs documenting the various native races of the empire. Consequently vast collections of portraits were commissioned or purchased, but the operation was never properly coordinated and even in the following years no other project was pursued in a systematic way. The photographers' motivations, both scientific and artistic, resulted in different approaches and degrees of thoroughness; however, their works show that many of them were quite conscious of the necessity of capturing the image of cultures that were entering a stage of rapid evolution and in some cases being disintegrated by the impact of an alien civilization and technology.

4

THE
AFRICAN
VENUS

Nigra sum, sed formosa:
The Ambiguous Conquest of Africa

J'aime le souvenir de ces époques nues.—BAUDELAIRE

Among the new horizons of the Dark Continent, photography discovered landscapes that had little to do with geography, and much to do with the forbidden dreams of the European middle class. Already in the eighteenth century, Africa was being thought of as the realm of the "loosest and corruptest women in the world," and Diderot saw it as "the lucky land where only Love is adored, where nothing else counts but pleasure, where customs are those of the golden age." Eroticism was naturally associated with the charm of that virgin land. In countries where the hot climate made clothes a hindrance, it was relatively easy to get models for study. As Diderot wrote, "On that continent the only known laws are those of nature, so that the ideas that Western prudery associates with certain objects are totally unknown,"[1] and the photographic nude, so shocking yet so desirable in the home country, with its still solidly rooted prejudices and sexual taboos, became a profitable business.

Whether he was an artist who had been living in Africa for some time or a conservative middle-class gentleman, the white man's vision was shaped by long-established stereotypes. From the Romantic literature of the nineteenth century we know the fascination that develops for a beauty that is cursed, insidious, and deadly, or undermined by profound physical and psychological malaise. Africa was compared to a beautiful and corrupt woman, and its supreme fascination lay after all precisely in this corruption, not only of moral but also of physical nature. No wonder, then, that the romantic "Ode to Consumption" begins with the verse "There is a beauty in woman's decay." Exoticism implied on the one hand admiration for the natives' beautiful bodies and traditional customs, and on the other hand horror inspired by their faces and rags. The white man was projected into a universe that appeared to him imbued with sensuality in all its aspects. From Shelley to Baudelaire, poets did not hesitate to profess their fascination with corruption and the tempting, contaminated, all-consuming beauty. It is interesting to note that this concept, which had disappeared in Europe by the end of the century, persisted in minor literature on Africa until well into the 1920s and 1930s.

In Africa the relationship between Beauty and Death appeared real and direct; Good and Evil, indissolubly linked, were seen as manifestations of one single primordial confrontation. Isak Dinesen wrote of Africa, "God and Devil are the majesty coeternal."

Fabulous from afar, shocking and horrible from close up, Africa seemed to deceive Europe, which felt sentimentally betrayed, scorned in its deepest feelings. And thus the theme of "lost illusions" was present everywhere. In this land, pervaded by strong voluptuousness and animal sensuality, the white man's rationality could be swept away, disgust and fear could be overcome by the twofold devastating charm of the African woman and the environment; this land was still too close to its primordial state, too lacking in cultural outlets, to offer an escape from the destructive course of desire. It could only be the object of a predatory and fatal adventure, as was as well the colonial undertaking itself. Sensuality was associated with cruelty and lust, and the relation between white man and native woman was similar to that between colonizer and colonized country, where exotic transgression was seen as a return to primitivism, to an immediacy of passion that Western custom had long since rejected.

The theme of black beauty and animality was rarely dissociated from that of stupidity and inferiority. One might almost say that the black woman was imagined without a head: The body is all that counts, a body offered to man's pleasure, an extremely simplified idea in which beauty is exclusively seen as underlining the erogenous zones of breasts and buttocks. The curves are abundant, the back is sumptuous, and the hips are magnificently shaped, while adolescent breasts blossom out on a superb, enticing bust.

Unfamiliar, violent sensations take hold of the white man in a place far removed from any control or inhibition by the civilized world. In sexual love between the white man and the black woman, Nature has the upper hand over civilization. Instinct is the only law, and desire predominates. All in all, it is only natural that the native woman has been one of the favorite topics of literature, either diaristic or fictional, and of figurative art, in particular photography: The artists and authors were men who saw women chiefly as erotic objects. And although they used a chaster language, the few female witnesses, such as Elena di Savoia and Isak Dinesen, had a similar attitude toward the African male, describing above all his physical beauty and strength, his "muscular arrogance."

As always, it would be wrong to generalize:

. . . in the brown, graceful daughters of the sun, blossoming like gentle flowers in those tropical greenhouses, there is still a softness of shape, a fullness of lines and a vague sweetness of expression, that violently lash one's blood by their intense, sharp, wild fascination as intoxicating as the perfumes and aromas of the resinous acacia bushes. Their beauty is refined and attractive, its charm completed by the eyes, which are large, soft, deep-black, shining and sometimes languid, eyes that always reveal intelligence and passion in lovemaking and that can set one shuddering and awaken unknown and violent emotions.[2]

For most "civilized" travelers the only point of reference was Europe, so that they all had the same stereotypical ideas about Africa. Only a few tried to formulate objective opinions, based on scientific investigation. As the new century drew nearer, the explorer's exceptional personality was replaced by the petit-bourgeois mentality of the bureaucrat, of the "little white man." Europe, becoming more and more moralistic and aseptic, continued to see itself as the model for every civilized society: Whatever was not Occidental was barbaric. Precise standards regulated the ethical, mental, and sexual behavior of the European middle class, and the African who did not agree to comply was considered an amoral savage.

The situation changed radically by the end of the nineteenth century, when following the military conquest a structured social organism began to establish itself in Africa: a hybrid caste system that, based on a European scheme, incorporated many indigenous elements. The foundations for this change were laid by the armed forces, the colonial military officers. They came from social classes that kept a ferocious eye on the virtue of their female relatives but also greedily read "licentious" works by Guy de Maupassant and Gabriele D'Annunzio. They did not find it too unpleasant to spend a few years in the colonies, where they could generously console themselves for having had to leave their country with its rigid customs.

A typical example can be found in a 1904 report by Gustavo Chiesi and Ernesto Travelli on the Italian Somaliland question:

Merriment was one of the characteristics of Governor Badolo's reign in the colony. Large supplies of wine and liquor were brought from Italy and in the Governor's office the work was often done with bottles and full glasses standing all over the desk. Drinking contests were won by those who managed to empty the highest number of glasses; in those conditions of semi-drunkenness and alcoholic excitement many things happened that were far from decorous and, for civil persons with self-respect, absolutely condemnable and indecent towards the natives. . . . Almost every night . . . light young women were brought in, almost all concubines of those gentlemen (the leading one was Big Fatima); they were made drunk on sparkling wines, champagne, hard drinks, and incited in their state of drunkenness to perform all kinds of obscenities accompanied by the singing and shouting of those officers, who lost all sense of self-respect or respect for others, all sense of human dignity.

As witnessed and related by the servants, the guards and the women who participated, those nightly orgies made extremely unfavorable impressions on the native notables, religious heads, merchants. As they were strictly religious and observant of Muslim laws they could only criticize such scandals, which offended their laws (especially against drunkenness) and destroyed any prestige, any distance between the white man and those loose black women who once were their own slaves and for whom those gentlemen paid ransom, not so much out of civil and humanitarian sentiments as for the purpose of making them objects for their own pleasure and to abandon them to common prostitution once they were tired of them or found younger and prettier girls. . . . Various times we heard of deplorable facts. For instance when a battleship reached Benadir, the residents in order to entertain the young officers when they came ashore, ordered their servants or guards to fetch some of the most beautiful local women and bring them to the Residence where some fun was going on. It is true that the women of those countries, especially of the Galla, Boran, Swahili, and Arab races, and even Somalians, are rather easygoing in prostituting themselves."[3]

Decades later, the Italian general Rodolfo Graziani, then commander of the troops in Cirenaica, issued a circular letter titled "Intercourse between officers and native women":

In less than one year I have been forced to repatriate four officers (one of them only recently) because they had paid ransom for native women (or had in any case approached them) in order to keep them as concubines or mistresses, which is practically the same thing. . . . Apart from any political considerations (concerning the speculation which the natives like to make on our affairs with their women), the disciplinary and moral side of the phenomenon is sufficient to condemn and despise it. . . . From a moral point of view let me remind you of the civil, economical and sometimes sentimental complications that occur when the woman becomes pregnant. . . . Headquarters and the Regional Authorities will do everything to meet this necessity by establishing—wherever possible—brothels in all the localities that are still without.[4]

The roots of the turbid sensuality that spread underground in nineteenth-century European society and emerged openly without shame in the colonies had already been formed in the eighteenth century. Diderot, by illustrating the customs of exotic populations, indirectly prepared the way for justification of sexual perversion. The Marquis de Sade must surely have read the travel reports by the first explorers and the *Supplément au voyage de Bougainville* by Diderot, and found inspiration in this literature. From the eighteenth century onward the idea developed of love as domination, total possession which became outrage and sometimes ended up in violence. This "different" sensuality inspired the morbid but very popular interest of the European in a typical institution of the Muslim countries: the harem. Whereas the black woman was seen as aggressive and dangerous but very active sensually, the harem was the expression of exhausted, subtly corrupt, and decadent sensuality. The harems, those secret castles of insolent voluptuousness, seemed to enclose in a labyrinth of dark passages and bright patios, in an elaborate prison of precious fabrics and perfumes, the rarest essence of passions of the voluptuous Orient—a fabulous world in which every detail is designed to stimulate the male's sensuality. In these erotic beehives, a mass of favorites, courtesans, and concubines wait for him in languid poses: opulent ebony-skinned goddesses in an aura of musk and patchouli, nude under their jewels; diaphanous creatures wrapped in velvet kaftans, their temples delicately tattooed and their feet dyed with henna. They smoke blond tobacco blended with strong narcotics; their eyelids are heavy and their hairstyles complicated. Surrounded by fumes of incense, they hatch subtle plots for intrigues and bloody conspiracies on whose results the destiny of entire populations may depend; they cultivate unimaginable corruptions and maddening desires.

Trying to disentangle concrete reality from the fantasy of those years is extremely difficult: There is little difference between travel journals, novels, and poems, because the traveler, overwhelmed by what surrounded him, was no longer able to distinguish among his own observations, his sensations, and visions. Literary memories, acute comments, unexpressed desires, forbidden fantasies were all weirdly entwined with living reality. In the second half of the century one of the typical contradictions of the colonial adventure manifests itself: On the one hand the white man feels he shares the proud identity of the Western world, which is at the peak of the Industrial Revolution and world conquest; on the other hand, with surprising ease certain codes and signs of behavior that characterize this very identity are discarded, like a garment that has suddenly become too tight.

As to the harem, a curious and picturesque episode is reported in the review *Fama*.[5] Horace Vernet, a famous orientalist painter of that time, had been invited by a Paris publisher to reproduce a series of views of Egypt by a revolutionary new technique invented the same year. Thus it was Vernet who had the honor, in 1839, of introducing photography on the African continent. As soon as he had landed in Alexandria and put himself under the protection of Vice-Regent Mehmet, Vernet began his work. The artist, as a true Romantic, went on his *excursions daguerriennes* wrapped in a wide Arabian cloak. This masquerade was so convincing that by a fortunate misunderstanding he was taken for an officer of the vice-regent's and, though no longer in his prime, managed to seduce one of his host's young slaves. Embarrassed though impassioned, he did not know quite how to handle the situation. But then, unwittingly to his rescue came the vice-regent himself, who had been seduced in his turn by photography. In fact, after his initial astonishment at its effects (as a good Muslim he had exclaimed, "It's the work of the Devil!"), he was so fascinated by the new technique that with Vernet's help he learned daguerreotypy. To win the admiration of the women of his harem, he decided to make a group photo of them. Owing, however, to various somewhat suspect chemical complications, the pictures did not come out and, so as not to lose face with the ladies, after much hesitation the vice-regent was forced to ask the French artist's assistance. And so Vernet could contemplate at his ease what others so doing would have paid for with their heads, if not more delicate parts. The resulting photos were, of course, kept by Mehmet.

Vernet's adventure was not unique. Although any contact was forbidden, illustrous travelers, writers, and above all painters seized any opportunity to become intimately acquainted with Islamic women. From Delacroix to Rochegrosse, exotic subjects seem to have offered a wonderful pretext for licentious works. Some painters indulged in scenes of sensuality mixed with violence, nudity associated with death—such as the famous *Death of Sardanapalus* by Delacroix or *La Justice du Chérif* by Benjamin Constant. Most preferred to evoke suggestive images of serene pleasure and passive beauties. Their works represent a vast and varied catalogue of harems, some exquisite (such as those by John Frederick Lewis, Jean-Auguste-Dominique Ingres, Gérome Chassériau), others picturesque, but quite a few very much like brothels. Examples are certain paintings by Amedeo Preziosi or Alphonse Etienne Dinet, up to Renoir's *Parisian in Algerian Costume*. The whole fashion trend was exotic and every *maison* offered its customers a Moorish girl dressed in wide pink trousers and a sequined bolero.

This fashion had addicts not only in the brothels: We know that George Sand smoked the hookah (the pipe used by Ingres's odalisques) and that in private she used to wear Arabian slippers and silk harem trousers, but judging from Liotard's portrait of the Countess of Coventry painted in 1749, Sand certainly was not the first one to adopt this fashion. Many artists, photographers, as well as painters, considered too bothersome the fatigue of traveling to the Orient and the difficulty of painting portraits on the spot, and preferred to find the "raw material" for their works in the home market. Ingres found his models for the famous *Turkish Bath* in Rome. Some years later, in Paris, specialized photographers supplied painters as well as connoisseurs of odalisques with a wide choice of portraits of generously shaped models, invitingly reclining on couches, sumptuously dressed in gossamer veils that concealed very little.

The beginning of the twentieth century brought gradual disillusion: As occidentalization progressed, sometimes at a forced pace, the Orient lost much of its mystic aura. Under the now worn-off veneer of exoticism appeared a different world, one of gloom, dreariness, and misery, but Europe still for a long time continued to imagine the Orient as a place of magic opulence, beauty, and mystery.

> *Les plus rares fleurs*
> *Melant leurs odeurs*
> *Aux vagues senteurs de l'ambre,*
> *Les riches plafonds,*
> *Les miroirs profonds,*
> *La splendeur orientale,*
>
> *Là, tout n'est qu'ordre et beauté,*
> *Luxe, calme et volupté.*[6]

5

NATURE

LANDSCAPE AND
THE NOBLE SAVAGE

Pre-Romanticism coincided during the last third of the eighteenth century with the foreboding inventions of the Industrial Revolution, with the consequent rapid evolution of rural scenery and an increase in the number of known lands and the consequent discovery of overseas nature. After the second half of the eighteenth century, the feeling for nature became an important theme in English literature. Herder, in a letter written in 1769, compared nature to a vital force, coming very close to Goethe's idea. The *Voyage de l'Ile de France* by Bernardin de Saint-Pierre, written in 1771, and the report by George Foster, a companion of Cook, published in English (1770), French (1778), and German (1779), helped increase the interest in exotic nature. It was only much later, however, that philosophical values were associated with uncorrupted nature, and at first only very hesitantly. The so-called *partie de campagne* fashionable in the eighteenth century had been an intellectual diversion of the aristocracy—a symbolic homage to Rousseau's noble savage—and had never gone beyond the perfectly tended lawns of the patrician villas on the road opened by the poetics of the sublime. The Romantic age "discovered" a wilder, less artificial nature, judging her a worthy background for the monologues of its great poets of solitude. Emerson was among the first to theorize the return to nature: "Nature is the artist's measure of comparison." In 1795 Schiller wrote his essay *On Naive and Sentimental Poetry*, where he placed nature as the main source for the aesthetic and moral inspiration of the then rising figure of the Romantic artist. Artists were "the guardians of nature. When they can no longer exert this function and feel in themselves the destructive influence of arbitrary and artificial forms, or have to fight them, they will appear as witnesses and avengers of nature. They will either become part of nature themselves or search for lost nature."[1]

At the beginning of the nineteenth century, the discovery of a much vaster geographic universe, productive efficiency multiplied by recent technological inventions, the renewed sense of nature—these together with a recovery of spontaneity formed a counterweight to all that was arid in the philosophy of the Age of Enlightenment and allowed for the possibility of a balanced situation of industrial optimism, open horizons, and peaceful exchanges among the various peoples.

At least this was the dream of the revolutionary idealists. Unfortunately, neither then nor later was Europe able to fulfill these promises. The rise of the machine occurred at the same time as the revival of a sense of nature in art and literature. Appreciation of wilderness and unspoiled scenery started in the chaos of the cities. Existing side by side, often in ambiguous intimacy and in spite of being violently opposed to each other, were spontaneity and demiurgic ideas, the former cultivated in sensations, the latter pursued in action; the former exalting individuals who had broken with their origins, the latter implacably propagating radical forms of progress and civilization.

And so, from the explorer to the conqueror, unbridled irrationality often goes hand in hand with shortsighted rationality. Great colonial empires were born; the bourgeoisie bought power and soon discovered it possessed the authority and force to ratify everywhere the dichotomy between exploited nature and a nostalgia for unpolluted wilderness. This intensified a contradiction for which there appeared to be no resolution. Naturalistic inspirations, technical efficacy, and the rush toward "differentness" had become irreparably dissociated. At the mutual dawn of Romanticism, industrialism, and extra-European empires, bourgeois power gradually started separating technique from the human factor, practical realization from sensitivity. As inspiration from nature and Promethean action developed along separate and parallel paths, a false humanism and pernicious unilateral universalism found a philosophical justification for the victorious failure of the ruling class's ideals. The European nations had already spoiled their lands and degraded their workers by hastily abolishing much of their past, all in the name of progress; perhaps as a logical consequence they also did so overseas, perverting the colonized populations and depriving them of their culture. The esthetic theme of wild lands to conquer and subdue was part of an impetus that comprised both the idea of rational exploitation of the unknown world and the concept of hopeful humanism.

Europe put her grip on Africa, with her plunder and her dreams: Virgin spaces and new men were the basic ingredients of one single effort in which the search for profit and creative delight were two inseparable motivations: The splendid anticipations of the triumphant march of civilization soon faded, and grand visions too often turned into the ugly reality of exploitation and pettiness. But at that time illusions were still fresh, and untamed nature was seen as a challenging enemy for this demiurgic effort. Perhaps an admirable enemy (because of obstinate resistance, enormous force, and, last but not least, overwhelming beauty), but yet an enemy to be slain. Seen from an objective viewpoint, the result of the battle might appear rather dubious. "Man dominates nature and is dominated by her. He is the being of Creation who not only resists nature, dominating her and evading her laws to satisfy his own needs, but moreover increases his control over her through his labor and will. Yet the assumption that the universe was created for him is far from being evident. Everything man builds is, like himself, ephemeral. Time fills up canals, cancels history and nations."

In the long run, man may always be a loser:

Nature takes no notice of man, nor of his work or his passage on earth. Whether he invents or builds astonishing objects or lives like a brute, nature remains indifferent. The real man is the savage who takes nature as she is. But as soon as man sharpens his intelligence, perfects his ideas and the means to express them, or acquires new needs and the means to satisfy them, he will realize that nature obstructs him in every possible way. Therefore he must strive to rape her, though she is certainly not less strong in resisting him. If man interrupts his work only one moment, nature immediately claims her rights by destroying, disfiguring, or undermining the very foundations of what her obstinate foe has realized, wiping out every trace of his transitory efforts. It almost seems as if she were impatiently putting up with the masterpieces created by human genius. The Pantheon, Saint Peter's in Rome, and all the marvelous creations of art—what are they all compared with the alternating of the seasons, with the movement of the stars, of the flow of the rivers, of the violence of the winds? An earthquake or the lava from a volcano will, sooner or later, do away with it all and the birds will build their nests among the ruins of those superb monuments, while the bones of their proud builders will be brought to light by the digging and scratching of wild animals.[3]

Most times man cannot understand what is happening and can only complain about adverse fate and unfortunate circumstances, being unable to grasp the intimate mechanism that rules nature's manifestations. It was therefore the responsibility of the artist, as much as of the scientist, to reveal and interpret nature's secrets. Botany, zoology, meteorology, geography, and geology emerged as distinct disciplines from the general indexes of natural history and philosophy. However, at the same time, science, philosophy, and art all pursued the same goal. Humboldt warned that it is necessary to study "physical phenomena not merely in their bearings on the material needs of life, but in their general influence on the intellectual advancement of mankind."[4] Goethe and Carus had seen empirical observation as a route to transcendental infinity; in fact, a major matter of conscience for the nineteenth-century artist was the practical relation between scientific knowledge and poetic truth. All exploratory expeditions to Africa included both scientists and artists—gathering, dissecting, describing, reproducing, rendering, and classifying animals, plants, and rocks. The urge to classify and label common to science appears also in the painting and photography of this period. From the general it was necessary to concentrate on the particular, in order to return to the general with a more mature understanding. Photography, as the other arts, gives different responses to different social, psychological, esthetic, and philosophical pressures. A photograph of a landscape can convey scenes of wild grandeur and at the same time, with its scientific certitudes, provide an exact visual encyclopedia of travel facts. Documentary edification and sublimity mingled to create the final work of art. Van Gogh in fact maintained that "art is man added to nature."

In a landscape the artist could choose to represent first of all those details that impressed him as most being in harmony with his sensitivity and temperament. Or he could also, and this would seem the easiest way when using photography, choose to reproduce nature objectively without trying to find in her the confirmation of an antecedent emotion, but with such realistic enthusiasm as to catch in the image her inherent poetry. Whether the picture reflected above all the sentiments of the artist or caught the impersonal poetry of nature, what really mattered was that it was able to provoke a recognizable emotion in the spectator, in other words that the picture should not be limited to reproducing a plain inventory of facts, but should be able to express something about the relationship existing between man and these facts.

Analysis of the African reality, to explain its exoticism, was carried out by codified European canons, accompanied, without being in contradiction, by a decided interest in what is least European, most different and exotic. At the same time exoticism verified the universality of European esthetic values. The very fact that the artist used these values to investigate, approve, or reject the various aspects of African reality, implied self-verification and confrontation. The artist used this esthetic experience for trying to understand what lay beyond the conventions of his own culture. But eventually this way of interpretation consisted mainly in decoding one's own sensations, even though it was claimed to be an intuition capable of penetrating everything, of passing through any cultural barrier.

In African scenery, where everything was nature and nostalgic suggestions abounded, return to the esthetic conventions of Western civilization became an unconscious but transparent goal. "As long as we were children of nature and nothing else, we were happy and whole; then we freed ourselves and lost both these qualities. Thence originates a double-faced and very different nostalgia for nature, nostalgia for her happiness and nostalgia for her completeness." As soon as one moves in her direction, leaving one's artificial sphere, nature immediately overwhelms us with her deep silence, with her "ingenuous" beauty and her "infantile" candor. The impact with unviolated nature creates nostalgia, distance, longing for the infinite; nature is felt as a pure and independent force, whole and boundless, and the talents of the artist who is near to nature are truly divine gifts: "Everything that nature achieves is divine."[5]

Nature lured the artist-explorer across compelling physical as well as spiritual frontiers, and the language used by travelers to describe the vast uncharted lands is an example, both in a figurative and literary way, of the complex mixture of themes, conventions, and associations this experience aroused. In 1876, on the bank of the Lualaba, Stanley wrote in his diary:

Downward it flows into the unknown, to the night-black clouds of mystery and fable. . . . Something strange must surely lie in the vast space occupied by total blankness on our maps. . . . [W]e have labored through the terrible forest, and manfully struggled through the gloom. My people's hearts have become faint. I seek a road. Why, here lies a broad watery avenue clearing the unknown to some sea, like a path of light![6]

The artist was also explorer, scientist, frontiersman, and minister. He ran arduous risks and suffered extreme hardships, but his very sufferings were accepted as a privileged mode of understanding the surrounding reality. His quest for beauty and terror led him through a nature unspoiled by man, purer and by implication seemingly closer to God. Mid-nineteenth-century esthetics could

hardly exist without the word "infinity," and nowhere else than amidst African primitive wilderness could its true sense better be intuited. In the presence of Nature, overwhelmed by her utmost grandeur, majesty, and beauty, the artist's deepest intentions were to unveil the arcane forces that regulate the universe, and to make everyone through his pictures aware of its laws.

Here we have to make a clear distinction between nature as revealed in European scenery and that of an African landscape. The European landscape is largely an expression of culture, the result of constant untiring human intervention, developed and stratified in the course of thousands of years. "Changeful in its beauty," Aldous Huxley wrote of Tuscany,

this wide landscape always preserved a quality of humanness and domestication which made it, to my mind at any rate, the best of all landscapes to live with. Day by day one travelled through its different beauties; but the journey, like our ancestors' Grand Tour, was always a journey through civilization. For all its mountains, its steep slopes and deep valleys, the Tuscan scene is dominated by its inhabitants. They have cultivated every rood of ground that can be cultivated; their houses are thickly scattered even over the hills, and the valleys are populous. Solitary on the hilltop, one is not alone in a wilderness. Man's traces are across the country, and already—one feels it with satisfaction as one looks out across it—for centuries, for thousands of years, it has been his, submissive, tamed, and humanised. The wide, blank moorlands, the sands, the forests of innumerable trees—these are places for occasional visitation, healthful to the spirit which submits itself to them for not too long. But fiendish influences as well as divine haunt these total solitudes. The vegetative life of plants and things is alien and hostile to the human. Men cannot live at ease except where they have mastered their surroundings and where their accumulated lives outnumber and outweigh the vegetative lives about them. Stripped of its dark woods, planted, terraced, and tilled almost to the mountains' tops, the Tuscan landscape is humanised and safe.[7]

But this very nature, forged by man and considered one of Europe's greatest attractions, produced very different reactions in those who had experienced the enlarged reality of broader landscapes, or were eager for other, more intense esthetic experiences. Such men were bored or even irritated and almost suffocated by the tiresome intimacy and the balanced beauty of a too orderly European nature. In his introduction to the novel *Allan Quatermain,* Rider Haggard describes his feelings: "No man who has for forty years lived the life I have, can with impunity go coop himself in this prim English country, with its trim hedgerows and cultivated fields, its stiff formal manners, and its well-dressed crowds."[8]

The discreet charm of the English landscape is swallowed up by the immense horizons and great solitudes; its delicate memory fades away when compared to the dark valleys resounding with roars and to the endless forests, the burning hot days and the wonderful nights of the African land. Africa is a land of overwhelming charm because everything is excessive, incommensurable, prodigious, incomprehensible, and, in short, inhuman. "And so in my trouble, as I walked up and down the oak-panelled vestibule of my house there in Yorkshire, I longed once more to throw myself into the arms of Nature. Not the Nature which you know, the Nature that waves in well-kept woods and smiles out in corn-fields, but Nature as she was in the age when creation was complete, undefiled as yet by any human sinks of sweltering humanity. I would go again where the wild game was, back to the savages, whom I love, although some of them are almost as merciless as Political Economy."[9]

Compared with the primordial energy emanating from the Dark Continent, ancient Europe, too long and too profoundly molded by man, seemed worn out and exhausted. Nature there had been irremediably tamed, and almost everywhere the landscape had lost the capacity to surprise. Everywhere the traces of man's incessant work were evident: Every gorge, inaccessible and forgotten though it might be, concealed some ruins, hundreds of years old; every valley had its village or its stinking factory; every hill was covered by vineyards or well-tended fields; behind every forest appeared a church tower; every gulf had a port and an arsenal. European man was both unprepared for and attracted by the deep

contrast between the cultural antiquity of the old continent and the violent and huge extension of Africa. The immensity and the wildness of Africa subjugated the colonizer. He was torn from his ship and thrown into a primitive canoe to travel upstream on rivers without end, or he was worn out by marches that took months and months. In spite of all these hardships white men slowly succeeded in transforming the lands they penetrated, but the final result was never a true copy of the Europe they had left behind: In fact it was a totally new product that could only be described as African. The white man's advance went hand in hand with an inevitable estrangement from European influence.

This is the reason why photography in Africa, though almost exclusively the work of Europeans, may be considered indigenous. The principles on which it is based are only partly imported and are generally developed according to criteria different from those adopted by contemporary European photography. Actually, a certain spirit in the way of taking pictures that had been developed in Africa (and not only in Africa but also in many overseas countries that shared the same frontier spirit) might even have had a considerable influence on European photography, thanks to the enormous diffusion of exotic photographs. It seems natural that the African experience should have induced the artist to undertake a closer research into nature and to make a more realistic description while photography in Europe was just at that time trying to imitate pictorial art. The artist felt that "raw" nature offered an alternative to the artfully picturesque, and the turn photography was taking at that moment might be compared with the phenomenon of so-called provincial art in painting. In fact the latter distinguished itself from the main body of painting by its fundamental primitivism. The starting point was the same for both movements and similar problems were dealt with, but in the end the results could not have been more different.

While the photographers' work sometimes triumphantly sustained the conventions of the picturesque, at other times it escaped them as extraordinary data pushed into their pictures with pragmatic authority. The immense extension of space, the giant mountains, the perennially dark forests and the blinding deserts, the forbidding and majestic scale of the land created baffling technical problems but also introduced a grander style in the rendering of landscapes that was the direct result of a deeper understanding of nature. The direct approach to nature favored the re-examination of the problems of composition with a fresh spirit, in which landscape photography led to a de facto realism that was not very different from Courbet's ideas. Nature dictates compositional structures with their own innate order and is totally indifferent to the traditional canons of art. While nature offers her own abundance and magnificence to the artist's sight and imagination, she also suggests the possibility of renewal, which allows the elaboration of original solutions of the landscape problem.

The spontaneous reaction to African light and air resulted in meticulous observation and rendering of details and was part of the photographer's and painter's overwhelming desire to make their works shine with the spirit of nature. Besides, the landscape photographer had to face certain problems that did not concern his colleagues specializing in studio portraits. Since its beginnings, portrait photography had rapidly developed conventional methods so that even someone without the slightest imagination and initiative was able to carry out the job mechanically and with acceptable results. But in outdoor photography the variability of the weather, temperature, and light conditions forced the photographer to face unforeseeable and extremely diverse situations.

Do not imagine, O my readers, that your artist kept down a diary of his feelings; he never could get beyond the second page of such a record: and there, at Philae, he had indeed other work. During his stay the rising sun saw him, encumbered with "baths" and bottles, scrambling up the bank from his dahibieh, by the base of this "Bed of Pharaoh"; and as the declining rays gilded its capitals, he was observed climbing frantically to the top of the great pylon, camera-frame in hand, to "use up" the last streak of light. They were hard days' work; but how delightful, how rich—to him—in their result![10]

Africa meant a journey backward in time that became more intense the more the traveler proceeded toward the heart of the continent. From the moment he landed, even in those countries of the African coast where European influence was felt most, life seemed to amble along in ancient ways and rhythms, forgotten in Europe many centuries ago, to such a point that Flaubert exclaimed, "Here is the Orient of the Middle Ages, of the Mameluks, of the Barbarians."[11] The interpretation of the exotic present was often confused with the re-creation of the past. When explorers penetrated the unknown lands of equatorial Africa, historical time, history itself, seemed to vanish. Africa, wrote Luigi Barzini in 1915, "had rudely torn me away from Europe, depriving my eyes and my mind of all that was familiar to me. Day after day I slipped down into a barbaric, patriarchal, ferocious past from which there seemed to be no return. From the day I had seen the last steamer, I had walked a long way back into the past. Riding through virgin lands I had moved backward through centuries that lay behind. What far, ancient, unspoiled world lay ahead of me?"[12]

The explorer and the artist experienced the passage from a biblical time, of which the majestic remains of Egyptian antiquity were reminiscent, to a geological time, to a past immemorial. The surface of the continent appeared shaped by the wash of rivers and oceans for eons inconceivable.

We were wanderers on prehistoric earth, on an earth that wore the aspect of an unknown planet. We could have fancied ourselves the first of men taking possession of an accursed inheritance, to be subdued at the cost of profound anguish and of excessive toil. . . . We were cut off from the comprehension of our surroundings. . . . We could not understand because we were too far and could not remember, because we were travelling in the night of first ages, of those ages that are gone, leaving hardly a sign—and no memories. . . . The earth seemed unearthly. We are accustomed to look upon the shackled form of a conquered monster, but there—you could look at a thing monstrous and free.[13]

There the stamp of man, unlike in European domesticated landscape or in North Africa, was as yet nonexistent, and nature appeared in its primordial virginity. Man had not yet penetrated Eden. Uninhabited nature suggested a remote and timeless antiquity. The land and scenery seemed to concretize the idea of the sublime. Yet sublimity has many faces.

Going up the river was like traveling back to the earliest beginnings of the world, when vegetation rioted on the earth and the big trees were kings. An empty stream, a great silence, an impenetrable forest. The air was warm, thick, heavy, sluggish. There was no joy in the brilliance of sunshine. The long stretches of the waterway ran on, deserted, into the gloom of the overshadowed distances. On silvery sandbanks hippos and alligators sunned themselves side by side. The broadening waters flowed through a mob of wooden islands; you lost your way on that river as you would in a desert, and butted all day long against shoals, trying to find the channel, till you thought yourself bewitched and cut off for ever from everything you had known once—somewhere—far away—in another existence perhaps. There were moments when one's past came back to one, as it will sometimes when you have not a moment to spare to yourself; but it came in the shape of an unrestful and noisy dream, remembered with wonder amongst the overwhelming realities of this strange world of plants, and water, and silence.[14]

When one observes nature, the most intense emotions are often aroused by unknown and surprising aspects of flora and fauna; solitude often accentuates feeling part of and understanding the landscape. The traveler is so much carried away by his contemplation of nature's scenery that he can no longer bear human presence. Even the native may become a disturbing element, especially if he is "bastardized," in other words when his poses and way of dress are more like those of a white man, so that he too becomes an alien element no longer in harmony with nature. The theme of silence and solitude, variously interpreted, runs through many accounts, as it does through many uninhabited photographs. Some photographers imposed their own artistic conventions on the natural scenery or tended to prefer views that recalled the European or arcadian landscapes they were used to, whereas others were exclusively interested in what appeared to them utterly exotic and "different."

Photographers captured landscape in pictures that could be enjoyed anyplace, and for a long time. Pausing to contemplate nature's beauty on the spot was rarely possible; most times it represented an unaffordable luxury as well as a real danger, and, anyhow, the expedition had to push on to reach its various goals. Also, the difficulty of the journey and the immensity of those lands made it very unlikely that the photographer would ever again have the opportunity of recording the same landscape. Civilization was soon bound to produce radical changes in many places and to destroy the scenery irremediably.

LEHNERT & LANDROCK
  (German)
Patio scene
gelatin silver print
Tunis, ca. 1900
Coll. Monas Hierogliphica, Milan

Attributed to FACCHINELLI
Genre scene with the pyramids in the background
Egypt, ca. 1880
Coll. Monas Hierogliphica, Milan

This image is particularly rich in references to the traditional models of Egyptian views (pyramids in the desert), but also to the European genre scene with the woman washing her clothes, and, on the right, the "beautiful beggar," a classic subject of Romantic painting.

85

LEHNERT & LANDROCK (German)
Desert scene
toned gelatin silver print
Tunisia or Algeria, ca. 1905
Coll. Monas Hierogliphica, Milan

Romantic views of the desert and Arabian fantasies adorned bourgeois homes. ". . . we crossed a caravan, the men wrapped up in the coufieh (the women totally veiled) on the dromedaries' necks; they pass by very close to us, we do not exchange a single word, they are like phantoms in the clouds. . . . It seemed to me, while the caravan was passing by, that the camels did not touch the ground, that they proceeded chest-on with a ship-like movement, that they were supported inside there and very high above the ground, as if they were walking in the clouds in which they sank up to the belly."

—*Flaubert, Notes de voyages, p. 241.*

Photographer Unknown
The Apostolic Vicar and an Orphan
gelatin silver print
ca. 1900
Coll. Archivio Provinciale dei Padri Cappuccini, Milan

"Now for the springing up of a new light in the dark land of dusky
Ham! Is there any power that will elevate the degraded race? Yes,
the Gospel-mighty power!"
                                    —*Alexander Mackay, C.M.S. Missionary, 1876*

(Photographer Unknown)
School for Natives, Missionary school in Massawa
photogravure
Eritrea, ca. 1900
Coll. Monas Hierogliphica, Milan

During the colonial period, schools in Africa were developed
through private gifts, through the support of missionary and other
societies, and through government initiative, but higher education
was not available until after the Second World War.

(Photographer Unknown) (Italian)
Singing Class with Teacher
toned gelatin silver print
Asmara, Eritrea, ca. 1900
Coll. Archivio Provinciale dei Padri Cappuccini, Milan

Public education, although highly developed in some colonies,
produced low-paid native clerks/white-collar workers for the large
European financial groups established in Africa and for the colonial bureaucracy.

(Photographer Unknown)
The Sons of the Cannibals Contemplating the Passion of the Redeemer
photogravure
Uganda, ca. 1910
Coll. Archivio Provinciale dei Padri Cappuccini, Milan

"These good people had indeed worshipped God without us. What does it matter that they worshipped Him in their own way . . . by eating man, or dancing in the moonlight, or wearing greegrees made of bark around their necks. Why should we insist on making them do things our way?"
—*Père Drumont in Mongo Bet,* Le Pauvre Christ de Banba (*Paris: Robert Laffont, 1956*), *p. 260.*

J. A. DA CUNHA MORAES (Portuguese)
The Band of a Great Fazenda
albumen
Angola, ca. 1870
Coll. Monas Hierogliphica, Milan

94

Fotografia COMINI · TESSENEI · N.183.B Asmara (Eritrea)

ALESSANDRO COMINI
    (Italian)
Tessenei
silver chloride print
Eritrea, ca. 1910
Coll. Marchesa Salvago Raggi

GIOVANNI DE SIMONI (Italian)
Tourists
Egypt, ca. 1910
Coll. Monas Hierogliphica, Milan

A well-known Italian journalist and amateur photographer, Luigi Barzini, in 1915, wrote that the same tourists who "can't forgive each other for running into each other reciprocally equipped with implacable Kodaks, and who deplore the very presence of the hotels where they were staying and of the Legations where they go for the slightest trouble," could not resist the temptation to have themselves photographed in groups under the sphinx or in front of the pyramids.

O L I V E R (British)
Engine Running First Mile, 21 June 1882
albumen
Mozambique
Coll. Monas Hierogliphica, Milan

The inventions and machines of the Industrial Revolution facilitated the consolidation and further expansion of the colonial empires. The difficulties in maintaining imperial control over enormous distances were reduced by the diffusion of steam power and of the telegraph. The remote outposts at the brink of darkness began relentlessly to multiply. The aimless violence of nature—be it catastrophes or the folly of primitive peoples—was increasingly confined within a dense network of railways and roads, the symbols of colonial penetration that influenced the pattern of political and economic development of Africa.

C. ECCLESIA (Italian)
*Portrait of explorer Luigi
    Robecchi-Bricchetti with
    Mabruk, a native child*
ca. 1890
Coll. Civici Musei, Pavia

This portrait demonstrates the influence of the European and African cultures on each other. Here the explorer and his young servant, both dressed as gentlemen, are riding their bicycles in a provincial Italian town.

VITTORIA SELLA (Italian, 1859–1943)
The Expedition Going Through a Vast Papyrus Swamp Between Mitiana
and Bujongolo
gelatin silver print
Uganda, 1906
Coll. Fondazione Sella e Istituto di Fotografia Alpina "Vittorio Sella"

"May 17. We wake up at 4 A.M. and though it is still dark the
caravan starts its march at half past five after the usual coffee or
chocolate, fried eggs, butter and biscuit. The march is uneventful
and crosses or runs along the side of rolling and grassy hills and a
few narrow and deep gorges. I take a picture of the marching
caravan."   —*From Vittorio Sella's travel diary*

VITTORIO SELLA (Italian, 1859–1943)
Alexandra Peak of Mt. Stanley
gelatin silver print
Uganda, 1906
Coll. Fondazione Sella e Istituto di Fotografia Alpina "Vittorio Sella"

"June 26. Unfortunately the fog came up from everywhere. I took rather convulsively a few photographs with my Kodak camera and then we went on with the larger camera up to the Alexandra Peak's ridge; we were surrounded by light fog and whipped by a strong and chilly SW wind. We found some comfortable rest and protection from the wind below a narrow ledge but only around 11 could we enjoy the warm and beneficial effect of the sun. A little earlier than midday I could take two photographs of the two highest peaks."

—*From Vittorio Sella's travel diary*

GIOVANNI DE SIMONI (Italian)
The Caliphs' tombs
Cairo, Egypt, ca. 1900
Coll. Monas Hierogliphica, Milan

On the southern side of the Citadel of Cairo, near the Mukattam range, is the city of the dead. It is a wide space of desert and rubbish, thickly interspersed with tombs and sepulchral mosques, mostly in a state of ruin. Of this necropole Eugène Fromentin wrote in 1869: "Those great mute monuments, deserted, a little more gilded than the sun, . . . lighter when the oblique rays fall on them, . . . reveal a flawless taste, with their walls striped a faded red, their inlaid domes, the few minarets delicately notched against the sky, they bear the most beautiful witness to the flowering of Arab genius."

Les ruines du Temple de Sphinx N° 17

ABDULLAH BROTHERS (Turkish)
The Sphinx's Temple Ruins
albumen
Egypt, ca. 1880
Private Coll.

Uniformity in dress, brought to civilized lands by the universal use of the black suit, was seen as a symbol of the leveling of social classes. Delacroix reflected in his diary on the greater modesty and beauty of Arab clothing: "Imagine what it is to see these consul-like characters lying in the sun, strolling in the street, or absorbed in arranging their babouches: people resembling Cato and Brutus, who do not even lack the haughty demeanor that those masters of the world must have possessed. These people own nothing more than the blanket in which they walk, sleep, and will be buried, and they have the air of satisfaction that Cicero in his curule chair must have had."

GUGLIELMO PLÜSCHOW (German)
Black and white nudes
ca. 1890
Coll. Monas Hierogliphica, Milan

It was no coincidence that when the forbidden dreams of the European bourgeoisie began at last to be translated into pictures, photographs showing various degrees of nudity were taken and eagerly collected. The camera permitted the owners of these "private collections" to vicariously participate in adventures that until then had been confined to the imagination.

LEHNERT & LANDROCK (German)
Tetuan. View of the Town from the Jewish Cemetery
photogravure
from the book *Picturesque North Africa*
Morocco, ca. 1910
Coll. Monas Hierogliphica, Milan

Centuries-old Jewish communities, many quite large, were spread throughout North Africa. Barely tolerated by the Muslim majority, Jews were permitted to live only in special quarters of Arab towns. In Morocco these were called "mellahs" and were under the sultan's own protection. Most Jews were forced to leave North Africa after independence or one of the early Arab-Israeli wars.

LEHNERT & LANDROCK
  (German)
Three veiled women
studio proof paper
Tunisia, ca. 1905
Coll. Monas Hierogliphica, Milan

A Muslim woman of a certain social
level was not allowed to go out or
to be seen by strangers. When she
did leave her house, she was veiled
from top to toe, and efforts to look
at her face were an extreme offense.

LEHNERT & LANDROCK (German)
"Ouled Nail" Dancing Girls
photogravure
from the book *Picturesque North Africa*
Algeria, ca. 1900
Coll. Monas Hierogliphica, Milan

The Ouled Nail, a nomadic tribe, would send their daughters into
the oases to earn their dowry. These strange "daughters of joy"
wore their whole fortune, partly in the shape of gold coins worked
into diadems and necklaces, partly in heavy silver ornaments.

Attributed to L U I G I   N A R E T T I
  (Italian, d. 1922)
Group of Danakils warriors
albumen
Eritrea or Somalia, ca. 1880
Coll. Monas Hierogliphica, Milan

(Photographer Unknown)
Masai
gelatin silver print
East Africa, ca. 1900
Coll. Museum für Völkerkunde, Vienna

The European photographer seemed
to find, in the immobility and the
dignified gestures of the African,
those lost gods that had been present
throughout the century in German
Romanticism, from Heine to
Nietzsche.

LEHNERT AND LANDROCK (German)
Eventide
albumen
Egypt, ca. 1900

Coll. Monas Hierogliphica, Milan

(Photographer Unknown)
Arab girl with a jug
albumen retouched with tempera
ca. 1880
Coll. Civici Musei, Pavia

In nineteenth-century Victorian
Europe, the very word "nude" was
emotionally charged. This photograph was originally of a bare-
breasted lady and so considered
unsuitable for publication. The
photograph was retouched with the
addition of a hand-painted blouse.

(Photographer Unknown)
Prisoners building a road
Algeria, ca. 1890
Coll. Monas Hierogliphica, Milan

While deportation and exile were the usual fate of defeated African
leaders, lesser prisoners often became a source of cheap labor.

LUCA COMERIO
(Italian, 1878–1940)
The hanging of an Arab "rebel"
Libya 1911
Coll. Monas Hierogliphica, Milan

A rare photograph of an execution.
Such documentation of a rather
common situation was often cen-
sored, as were images of slavery,
famine, or death in battle.

(Photographer Unknown)
Blockhouse in Ghardaia
Algeria, ca. 1890
Coll. Monas Hierogliphica

116

GIOVANNI DE SIMONI (Italian)
War dance
Eritrea, ca. 1905
Coll. Monas Hierogliphica

"It would, I think, be untrue to say that [the African volunteer troops] gave their lives to uphold the British Empire, for that was a conception beyond their understanding . . . their chief motives were, I think, personal love of their officers, the terms of pay offered, the decorations they hoped to win, ignorance of the conditions of warfare to which they would be exposed, and their natural courage and love of adventure."

—*Capt. F. J. D. Lugard*

LEHNERT & LANDROCK (German)
Monks with Lioness in South Oran
photogravure
from the book *Picturesque North Africa*
Algeria, ca. 1900
Coll. Monas Hierogliphica, Milan

MAURO LEDRU (Italian)
Massaua Danakils at Camp Gherrar
albumen, from the book *Ricordi di Massaua,* 1885
Eritrea, 1885
Coll. Monas Hierogliphica, Milan

Left
LEHNERT & LANDROCK
(German)
Girls in a Tunis patio
hand-colored gelatin silver print
Tunisia, ca. 1905
Coll. Monas Hierogliphica, Milan

Romantic literature fostered a strereotype of the Arab woman, and especially of the harem, perceived as the manifestation of an exhausted, subtly corrupt, and decadent sensuality. In fact, there was no institution at once so familiar and so misunderstood as the harem, owing to the secrecy that surrounded it and the impossibility of obtaining firsthand information. In Islam, woman's segregation was almost complete, and photographers and painters had in most cases to use Jewish women dressed as Muslims or courtesans.

Right
LEHNERT & LANDROCK
(German)
Boy and girl
studio proof paper
Tunisia, ca. 1905
Coll. Civici Musei, Pavia

While photographs like this one were often banned by colonial authorities, they found wide distribution in Europe. The white man was projected into a universe imbued with sensuality. Eroticism was a natural component of the charm exerted by this mysterious and exotic land.

LEHNERT & LANDROCK (German)
Kairuan
photogravure
from the book *Picturesque North Africa*
Tunisia, ca. 1910
Coll. Monas Hierogliphica, Milan

"Instead of our misty sky, we have the sparkle of a hot clear sky in
    which vultures are circling; instead of grey houses, the ramparts,
    the domes, and the minarets of the Arab town rise with a copper
    glow in the scorching sun."
    —Théophile Gautier, *Exposition de Tableaux Modernes,* Paris, 1860

6

PROGRESS

THE MACHINE
AND GREAT
ENGINEERING WORKS

Photography in general seemed an inadequate way to record the immense majesty and wildness of the landscape. Landscape photography was seldom able to express the menace of nature, the terror of plague, fever, the never dying winds, the rivers' incessant flowing through the forests, the ever present threat of death. A reassuring and optimistic vision prevailed instead, almost hinting that, sooner or later, the forces of nature were bound to be harnessed by the demiurgic action of man. The inventions and machines of the Industrial Revolution facilitated the consolidation and further expansion of the colonial empires. The difficulties in maintaining imperial control over enormous distances were reduced by the diffusion of steam power and of the telegraph. The remote outposts at the borders of darkness were inevitably bound to multiply. The aimless violence of nature—be it meteoric events or the barbarian folly of primitive people—was being confined within an increasingly dense network of railways and roads.

Progress left continuously deeper marks on the natural environment: The artificial scenery it created, the torments and wounds it inflicted upon the soil go hand in hand with the exploitation of the natives. As long as the Negro was of no definite economic interest he was considered a noble savage who acted as an extra in the performance of untamed nature. As soon as the exploitation of the natural resources became feasible and profitable, the noble savage was dead. What remained was an incomprehensible "ferocious animal" to be fought when it got in the way of the march of progress, to be eliminated when it could not be tamed or otherwise exploited.

In Africa, the new constructions of industrial technology—bridges, dams, railways, factories, and mines—had lasting consequences. From the development of river navigation to the introduction of irrigation works, the country was irreversibly altered, producing strong contrasts. It took some time for photographers to give up their original ideas of what Africa looked like and accept the changes that were taking place, to see them as interesting topics. For the commercial photographer the growing cities and commercial centers not only offered the largest market for his work, whether portraiture, landscape, or architectural views, but also supplied a readily available subject matter: Photographs illustrating the spread of cities, notable new buildings, and other indicators of civic pride found a steady sale to visiting travelers and to settlers to send back to Europe.

According to the structure of the land, either the railway or the river steamboat is the symbol of colonial penetration. So the elegy composed by Kipling in *.007* is by no means surprising: "A locomotive is, next to a marine engine, the most sensitive thing man ever made." To Joseph Conrad, even a small and very decrepit steamer foretold the European's drastic and enduring impact on Africa, incredibly out of proportion with the modest, almost pitiful appearance of this instrument of progress: "The long reaches that were like one and the same reach, monotonous bends that were exactly alike, slipped past the steamer with their multitude of secular trees looking patiently after this grimy fragment of another world, the forerunner of change, of conquest, of trade, of massacre, of blessings."[1]

Only a few romantics persist in traveling the traditional way, although there is no more need for it: "Poor Luxor! All along the river banks are moored those tourists' boats, a kind of barracks two or three storeys high, which these days infest the Nile, from Cairo upstream as far as the cataracts, and their hoarse sirens hiss while their

engines are continuously running making an intolerable noise. . . . Where shall I ever find a quiet place to moor my Dahabieh without having to contend with officials from Cook's Agency?"[2] Loti admired the Sultan of Morocco for wanting "neither Parliament nor Press, nor railways or roads" in his country and for his quiet and noble contempt for modern turmoil. But a few nostalgics are not sufficient to stop progress; Europe lands in Africa and destroys it. Already fifty years earlier, Flaubert, who had preceded Loti along the same itinerary, complained: "It's very ravaged and damaged, not by the course of time, but by tourists and scholars."[3]

If telegraphy enormously helped the far-flung parts of empires to keep in touch with one another, it is also true that in some cases the railways were considered a major propellent toward political unity. The railroad was, for instance, a crucial factor in influencing the pattern of political and economic development in South Africa, and it was the extension of railways to the interior of Nigeria that facilitated the administrative union of the northern and southern parts of the colony in 1914, while on the eastern side of the continent the Uganda Railways had been built as an important means of holding together the great British East Africa Protectorate, from the sea coast to the Victoria Nyanza. The Uganda Railroad (1896–1901) ran east to west, but there had also been a plan for a railroad running south to north. "Cape to Cairo" Grogan undertook a two-year walk in 1898–99—from one end of Africa to the other—to study the feasibility of such a railroad. This was the dream of Cecil Rhodes, who saw it as the spine of a great British Africa, connecting the Cape and the Mediterranean, bringing commerce and settlers and civilization into the heart of the continent. As with so many other African dreams that failed to materialize, the railroad was never completed.

After having documented the supreme beauty and immensity of the African scenery, the European photographer recorded man's penetration, modification, and finally possession of nature through his great engineering works. These works represent the victorious myth of progress that celebrated its triumphs in Europe, from the Crystal Palace of 1851 to the Eiffel Tower of 1889; they are, at the same time, a symbolic assertion of supremacy: The Great Beast was being tamed by the building of artificial landscapes. Modern man seems to agree with Witelo when he states that "artificial things are more beautiful than natural ones."[4] Man and machine cannibalized nature, and photography documented the process. The machinery, the treaties, the railroad tracks, the building of new cities and harbors, testified to the unlimited powers of civilization, their geometries projecting the infinite resources of the Mind. To contemporary eyes, they incarnated the energy of progress itself. Men of resources were building the future for a price as yet undetermined, charting infinity with maps and roads, schools and prisons, forts and churches.

The poses of the white man in a landscape where the violation of the environment is already manifest and irreversible can be read as signifying the terms by which he defines its tenancy in the world. Whereas explorers and traders tried to keep a low profile, soldiers, missionaries, engineers, and settlers strove to modify the environment and were utterly proud of their achievements. They are often portrayed in the middle of a devastated and ravaged landscape, of a leveled nature stripped of her distinctive features, a nature where man's mark is everywhere.

7

THE WHITE MAN'S
VISION OF HIMSELF
AND THE
CHANGED AFRICAN

In the middle of the nineteenth century, and for almost another hundred years, Africa was for Europeans a challenge without strict life rules, in which one relied only on one's own intelligence, force of character, willpower, and faith. Resolute, young, eager, wholehearted, strong men faced Africa: solitary explorers full of enthusiasm and illusions spurred by their passion for the unknown and for risk, ready for great brave enterprises and great sacrifices. The reward was suffering and sometimes death. A myth was about to be born.

The intrepid white hunter cuts through the thick vegetation with his chest and makes his way through the jungle, sure of his rights, inflexible in his determination. Beside him is a faithful native of that wild country who carries the spare rifle. Beyond the tangled mass of exotic plants and vines appears the form of a temple erected to an unknown goddess.

    Silent wild animals guard these ruins as they have from time immemorial, while in quiet pilgrimage men and women of the jungle approach the temple to bring precious gifts which the goddess accepts with hieratic indifference. When the intrepid hunter passes the barrier of ferocious beasts and overcomes the obstacle of the fanatic worshippers, to find himself face to face with the glacial beauty of the priestess, the miracle of love explodes. The white hero is tall and virile in his tropical outfit with the shirt sleeves rolled up, a bright kerchief around his neck, high boots, breeches, and of course the inevitable heavy belt sagging down on the right where he carries his revolver. The native by his side is silent and inscrutable, dressed decently and with a turban that gives him an aura of mystery. He is the touch of local color and the white hero's shadow.

Such a figure might be the leading character of any number of adventure stories, novels, and later of movies or comic strips inspired by them. He had his gladiatorial youth in the last years of the last century, came to glorious maturity in the period embracing the First World War, and died in the 1950s when other heroes appeared, from the 007's with their license to kill, to the various Supermen, who, however highly unlikely, managed to seem much more credible than this lone explorer whose lost jungles had by then become the theater of increasingly cruel wars.

But still a century ago, the travels made to discover the great geographical mysteries had, like all epics, their own mythology, rich in characters and places able to stir the imagination of an immense bourgeois public, which stayed safely at home but was very keen on exoticism. The heroic gesture is often closely linked to the idea of martyrdom, and the explorer's often tragic end, his supreme sacrifice for the sake of science and civilization, is considered the logical conclusion of an intense existence, certainly a fine conclusion for someone who dies while defending such sacred ideals. His travel diaries with his extraordinary adventures and his terrible toils capture the general interest, and his reports always turn into great literary successes: best sellers, continuous reprints, publication in all the major European languages. The narration of his hardships attract the morbid interest of the daily press and illustrated weeklies. They are converted into widely read articles written in a rather pompous style, but not without a certain charm and suggestiveness, which from the pages of the magazines incite the reader to direct action, sometimes to popular participation, new crusades.

The names of Mungo Park, Denham, Clapperton, Bruce, Speke, Grant, the Lander brothers, and many others became known to the general public and prepared the way for the most famous epic hero of all: the "good doctor" David Livingstone, champion of the victims of the slave trade. Livingstone's counterpart will be Henry Morton Stanley, a journalist by vocation who became an explorer by profession, the one who, as everybody knows, found the good doctor after the latter's disappearance in the heart of Black Africa. The epoch of African exploration is full of illustrious duels and rivalries, which divided the public's heart and filled history to the brim with heroes. A typical example is Burton and Speke's "Nile Duel" at a time when the exact location of the great river's sources was a mystery that held the whole world under its spell. But Livingstone and Stanley are also two legendary figures who can be adopted as the emblems of two different generations and ways of interpreting and living the African adventure. The image of the true Christian embodied by Livingstone is the stereotypical picture that missionary propaganda has helped create. The white man is an apostle of civilization, more virtuous than Cato, unshakable of purpose, yet deliberate and moderate in his actions, his heart full of love for his unlucky black brothers who still dwell in darkness, his heart full of horror toward any useless violence. In January 1866, Livingstone penetrated for the last time the heart of the continent and although he did not realize it, he discovered Lake Tanganyika, "the source of the sources." However, for two long years, Livingstone disappeared, and back in the civilized world people regarded him as missing and perhaps dead. Incredible stories made the rounds about him, that he had "gone native" and had married a black princess. Livingstone was found by the young New York *Herald Tribune* reporter Stanley, who had cleverly prepared the phrase "Dr. Livingstone, I presume?" beforehand. Stanley was certainly not inspired by sentimental Christian mysticism; he believed in the cult of the power of conquest, as expressed in the works of writers like Kipling.

The European imagination had suddenly grasped the vastness of the colonial empires, and the responsibilities involved. Moreover, Romanticism and the decadent Aesthetic Movement had run their course, and it was into this gap that an exotic realism aggressively and triumphantly stepped, striking new chords of duty, patriotism, and military preparedness, which today we could call imperialism and militarism. Stanley started his career almost by chance, out of a romantic sense of adventure, to express his exuberant vitality, to fight his way free of the dreariness of everyday life. He was only twenty-eight years old and already a top journalist when his newspaper charged him with the African expedition. Not very tall, but sturdy and in excellent condition, he had a large mustache, gray eyes, and thick chestnut hair parted on the right. His style was that of a braggart, romantic, rough, and ambitious, but he was a man who seemed able to get safely out of any hazardous situation. Stanley the demigod, with his feet firmly on the ground, was interested in everything, and managed to bend everything to his will. Whether he was hunting wild animals or hostile natives, he would describe the incident in a studiedly boastful style: "My elephant rifle was loaded with explosive balls for this occasion. Four shots killed five men and sank two canoes. The two others retired to assist their friends out of the water. They attempted nothing further."[1]

The rifle was rapidly replacing the Bible, and by now half a century had passed since the times of the many proselytes and the few who were willing to face adventure alone. The stories by the first explorers, Kipling and Stevenson, had worked; by now many were attracted to the primitive frontier lands. When Stanley decided to find men to accompany him on his second expedition, volunteers abounded. As he remembered: "Over 1200 letters were received from generals, colonels, captains, lieutenants, midshipmen, engineers, commissioners of hotels, mechanics, waiters, cooks, servants, somebodies and nobodies, spiritual mediums and magnetizers, etc., etc. They all knew Africa, were perfectly acclimatized, were quite sure they would please me, would do important services, save me from any number of troubles by their ingenuity and resources, take me up in balloons or by flying carriages, make us all invisible by their magic arts, or by the science of magnetism would cause all savages to fall asleep while we might pass anywhere without trouble."[2] It seems natural, almost obvious, that the three men selected were not among those who had written, but two brothers, Edward and Frederick Pocock, who were Kentish fishermen and boatmen, and Frederick Baker, a desk clerk at the Langham Hotel in London.

When Stanley came back to Europe after the Congo exploration, he wrote: "I discovered that I was getting more and more unfit to what my neighbors called civilized society."[3] Piaggia feels like a stranger in his own country and "thinks he cannot worthily conclude his life outside the land he has given the best and dearest part of his life."[4] Many knew they had left in Africa a piece of their soul. Isak Dinesen wrote:

If I know a song of Africa—of the Giraffe, and the African new moon lying on her back, of the ploughs in the fields, and the sweaty faces of the coffee-pickers, does Africa know a song of me? Would the air over the plain quiver with a colour that I had had on, or the children invent a game in which my name was, or the full moon throw a shadow over the gravel of the drive that was like me, or would the eagles of the Ngong hills look out for me?[5]

As disinterested exploration, out of love for adventure or science, came to an end, travelers and scientists became more and more the conscious instruments of economic interests, and their enterprises became a screen for the quite concrete goals of those who wished to assure and consolidate the "rights" of occupation and exploitation of the newly discovered regions. In a few years the explorer was replaced by others better suited to the new time. The European powers had begun to occupy the African territories by military force and to impose on the natives political systems alien to them. The official iconography then spread the images of those men who were to become the columns of the great colonial empires: the soldier, the civil servant, and, lastly, the settler.

In a period of relative peace in Europe, overseas the

military often seized total control of the colonial operations, as if it had adopted the theory of Gumplowicz that social progress depends exclusively on racial struggle and the extermination of the defeated foe. Some went completely haywire and established personal short-lived empires, refusing any control by the mother country or even by the military hierarchy. Kurtz in *Heart of Darkness* is emblematic: "His very existence was improbable, inexplicable, and altogether bewildering. . . . It was inconceivable how he had existed, how he had succeeded in getting so far, how he had managed to remain—why he did not instantly disappear. 'I went a little farther,' he said, 'then still a little farther—till I had gone so far that I don't know how I'll ever get back. . . . '"[6]

They were buried under the enormous weight of colonial loneliness. There was never more than one step between damnation and redemption. When someone lives for years without seeing another of his kind, when he has to talk to his mirror to keep from going round the bend, a strange and lasting relation is born between the environment and the stubborn man who mastered it. Apart in his triumph he stands, a lone friend of the "Furthest Shack of the Never-Never Land" (Kipling). Whereas some stood out above all for the incredible atrocities they inflicted on the native populations, others profited from their isolation in a more discreet way. Their role was that of an individualistic hero, snubber of conventions, cultivated, above all the holder of a limitless power. Toward the end of the last century, de Maupassant visited some of the more isolated military outposts in the southern Algerian Sahara; although they were in charge of controlling immense territories, the commanding officers had only rare contact with their superiors and were completely cut off from the relatively civilized life of the coastal settlements. "The commanders of the outposts considered themselves true omnipotent monarchs; . . . living alone, they have read much, are educated and erudite, and good conversationalists; living alone in this vast desolate country with its boundless horizons, they are able to think like solitary laborers."[7] Captain Bottego,

speaking firsthand, gives us an idea of their feelings, describing Africa as "the country of freedom, where a man, finding himself under abnormal conditions of life, can measure his own and other men's capacities and learn to get a better insight into human nature."[8]

Solitary heroes, of course, were not Europe's only export. Daudet and de Maupassant were among those who denounced the big swindle by unscrupulous merchants and speculators hidden behind the colonial adventure." De Maupassant called Algiers "Europe's drain for the so-called civilized races . . . ; France dumps there everything that is obsolete, the world vomits there its adventurers."[9]

Conrad used language just as plain in describing the representatives of civilization in the Congo: "Their talk was the talk of sordid buccaneers: it was reckless without hardihood, greedy without audacity, and cruel without courage; there was not an atom of foresight or of serious intention in the whole batch of them, and they did not seem aware these things are wanted for the work of the world."[10] Nor is Céline very indulgent toward the colonial undertaking:

the resident traders seemed to thieve and prosper more easily than in Europe. Not a coconut or a groundnut throughout the whole territory escaped their depredations. The civil servants realized, as they grew more tired and ill, that they'd been done in the eye when they were sent out here and weren't getting anything after all except braid, and forms to fill up, and practically no salary at all. So they glowered at the traders. The military group, which had fallen even lower . . . , merely existed on a diet of imperial prestige, helped down with a lot of quinine and miles and miles of regulations.[11]

Most of the Europeans in Africa were "petits blancs" ("little whites"), as the French called them, there to earn their bread and a little butter, but perhaps it is these who are the true protagonists of the colonial period: insignificant bureaucrats and shopkeepers who, suddenly gone mad, took themselves for conquerors of empires. Far from any control and terms of comparison, these members of the "master race" delighted in the incivility and ferocity that are latent in every form of idealism and gave vent to the sinister instincts hidden within the folds of noble intentions.

To the writers of negative exoticism, the colonial enterprise became an unforgivably absurd adventure, which allowed fringe sectors of bourgeois society to explode into the worst kinds of misdeeds, sooner or later to meet their well-deserved destruction in God-forsaken countries with unpronounceable names, among peoples with whom physical and moral violence seemed to be the only possible form of intercourse.

Photography was used in Africa to define and propagate the popular image of the white man as conqueror and civilizer, presenting him as explorer, soldier, hunter, missionary, or master of the machines produced by victorious Western technology. Throughout the Victorian era, the building of railroads and proliferation of the steam locomotive had particular iconographic importance. The train as a symbol of progress and modernity was one of the leitmotifs of European propaganda until the end of the nineteenth century. Especially in landscape photography, the white man and his machines signify the terms by which the age defines his tenancy of the world. Depicting himself in the wilderness, the colonial is diminished but never overwhelmed. Though often enveloped by theatrical drama, the white man seems rather indifferent to the large natural dramas he witnesses, and rare are the photographs in which he seems engaged in some sort of dialogue with the surrounding wilderness. This does not so much indicate a total alienation between civilized man and nature (deeply appreciated and respected by many photographers) as emphasize the white man as an element basically unrelated to his African surroundings. The landscape appears to be, or actually is, a mere painted backdrop against which the European assumes worldly poses, appearing busily and importantly absorbed in daily tasks. Rarely seen unself-consciously, he is often photographed in a studio full of classical architectural props, papier-mâché rocks, and potted palms. The photograph will pass him on to future generations clean-shaven, well-laundered, and showing off all the paraphernalia popularly attributed to the explorer, from the pith helmet to the rifle, the fieldglass and the towering rucksack.

A number of other portraits show the white man in an opposite disguise, in African dress and environment. This masquerading is confined to Muslim attire and customs, however, for the areas below the Sahara held no cultural allure for Europeans. Sometimes even Disneyland-style decor was used, with sarcophagi, mummies, and Egyptian statuettes. Ironically, almost all of those portraits were made in Africa.

A series of portraits of the explorer Luigi Robecchi-Bricchetti might constitute an exhaustive sample of the extremes brought about by the refusal to follow the standard, uniform poses practiced in European photographic studios. In one portrait by Luigi Fiorillo, a photographer in Alexandria, Robecchi-Bricchetti and a woman companion appear locked in a sarcophagus, which brings to mind Theophile Gautier, who exclaimed: " as for me, nothing would excite me more than a mummy."[12] In another photograph the same traveler appears as a Bedouin standing in front of a backdrop painted to suggest a desert landscape with rocks and a few palms. The Africa hinted at by an assembly of bogus and heteroclite objects became a theatrical stage where the achievements of the characters were played out. The exotic disguise was a declaration of originality in which revolt, narcissism, and exhibitionism all played a part. For this reason the intellectuals expressed disgust for modern garments; Loti was drastic in his condemnation "of the clothes of our narrow-minded and wicked century. Here everybody wears a uniform, gray coat, hat or cap,"[13] and he recalled the opinions of Baudelaire, Huysmans, and Montesquiou. Jean Lorrain confirmed these: "Oh, this modern costume and the clumsiness of the human body in the clumsiness of these stiff garments that are supposed to be a man's ideal outfit!"[14]

The reverse of the European masquerading in African dress shows the black (here again, not the Arab) in European clothes; once more the ferocity of ridicule is used to emphasize the inferiority of the subjugated race. The first European travelers found the naked inhabitants natural and beautiful, although sometimes rather indecent. Nonetheless, they were seen as savages, and it was the white man's duty to bring the light of civilization to his unfortunate brothers, teaching them to behave properly, even in the matter of dress.

In every part of the world, clothes express social and cultural status and have, therefore, a symbolic value; but fine feathers do not always make fine birds, and sometimes what should be a symbol of progress becomes only an image of degradation. In Africa, wherever European culture was imposed, the disintegration of indigenous societies and the loss of cultural memory and oral traditions may constitute the most serious damage endured by the subdued populations. Everything the Africans have learned about their history they have read in books written by Europeans, so that it might seem that without the Europeans Africa would never have had a history. The tragedy of the colonized peoples consists above all in this loss of their cultural identity, aggravated by their unsuccessful assimilation into the civilization imposed on them by the West.

The fact that the civilizers were unable to recognize themselves in the "dark mirror" of the native who had adopted their customs and habits is one of the major internal contradictions of the "great" work of civilization—a contradiction wherein lies a major reason for the failure of the acculturation policy. The ambivalent reaction of the European faced with an African who wears Western-style clothes is very revealing. The white man has never been able to see in this "civilized" black anything more than a pathetic or amusing creature, an unfaithful reflection of himself. To accept the white man as a model is of course praiseworthy and right, but the result is considered a caricature or, even worse, interpreted as an unjustified claim to equality. On the one hand, clothes are thought of as a vice introduced by the white man. The black is beautiful only when he is naked. As always, the contradiction is total: To the white man the fact that the black covers his nudity implies a sense of shame and is, therefore, an oblique reflection of the latter's morbid sensuality and innate amorality, whereas formerly his nakedness was considered the expression of a still uncorrupted naturalness. At the same time, there is no doubt that wearing clothes is a result of civilization and therefore must undoubtedly be a positive fact, and certainly the blacks' degree of civilization is measured also according to his way of dressing. And so the white man is caught in a dilemma of his own making. Whether he decides to bring civilization or not, he is apparently unwilling to accept the consequences of his actions and so whatever he does is wrong.

LEHNERT & LANDROCK
(German)
Tunisian Bedouin woman with child
photogravure
from the book *Picturesque North Africa*
Coll. Monas Hierogliphica, Milan

LEHNERT AND LANDROCK (German)
Mamelouk Tombs Through a Gateway
albumen
Egypt, ca. 1900
Coll. Monas Hierogliphica

(Photographer Unknown)
Dentist at the Market
studio proof paper
Asmara, Eritrea
Coll. Archivio Provinciale dei
  Padri Cappuccini, Milan

VITTORIO SELLA (Italian, 1859–1943)
Ford of the Wimi River
gelatin silver print
Uganda, 1906
Coll. Fondazione Sella e Istituto di Fotografia Alpina "Vittorio Sella"

In 1846, the *Art Union Journal* of London urged that the camera should "be henceforth an indispensable accompaniment to all exploring expeditions," and it advocated that "by taking sun pictures of striking natural objects the explorer will be able to define his route with such accuracy as greatly to abbreviate the toils and diminish the dangers of those who may follow in his track." This opinion must have been shared by the Royal Geographical Society, which appointed John Thomson instructor of photography to teach African explorers to keep accurate visual records of their travels.

GIOVANNI DE SIMONI
  (Italian)
Cruise on the Nile
Egypt, ca. 1910
Coll. Monas Hierogliphica, Milan

Occupation, colonization, Western-
ization, and the gradual improve-
ment of travel and facilities in foreign and distant lands made them
increasingly accessible to European
travelers and artists. By 1868
Thomas Cook had established tours
to Egypt that took travelers as far as
Aswan with fairly good hotels in
Cairo as early as 1840.

Left
Attributed to LUIGI NARETTI
   (Italian, d. 1922)
"Madame"
albumen
Eritrea, ca. 1885
Coll. Monas Hierogliphica, Milan

The "madame" were temporary
wives or prostitutes. Note that the
women are wearing only jewels, in
contrast to their miserable everyday
condition underlined by the bleak-
ness of the furnishings.

Right
WILLIAM D. YOUNG (British)
Swahili warrior
toned silver print
Kenya, ca. 1900
Private coll.

J.A. DA CUNHA MORAES (Portuguese)
On the Banks of the River Chiloango
albumen
Angola, ca. 1870
Coll. Monas Hierogliphica, Milan

J. A. DA CUNHA MORAES (Portuguese)
Banana Plantation
albumen
Loanda, Angola, ca. 1890
Coll. Monas Hierogliphica

The poses of individual white men in a landscape where the violation of the environment is already manifest signify the terms by which they define its tenancy in the world. Explorers and traders tried to keep a low profile, but soldiers, engineers, and settlers wanted to modify the environment and took enormous pride in their achievements. Here they are portrayed amid a leveled nature stripped of her distinctive features, a nature where man's mark has been deeply imprinted.

Left
RICHARD BUCHTA
Arab Woman
albumen
Sudan, ca. 1875
Coll. Museum für Völkerkunde, Vienna

Right
(Photographer Unknown)
  (Jesuit Missionary)
Newlyweds
photogravure
Congo, ca. 1910
Coll. Monas Hierogliphica, Milan

European clothing was thought to
show the civilizing effect of missionary work. But the civilizers were
seldom able to recognize themselves
in the "dark mirror" of the native
who adopted their customs and
habits. The ambivalent reaction of
the European faced with an African
in Western-style clothes is very
revealing. The typical white man
was unable to see in this "civilized"
black anything more than a pathetic
or amusing creature, an unfaithful
reflection of himself: To accept the
white man as a model was of course
praiseworthy and right, but the
result is considered a caricature or,
even worse, interpreted as an unjustified claim to equality.

COUTINHO BROTHERS
African lady
toned silver print
Zanzibar, ca. 1890
Coll. Civici Musei, Pavia

A. C. GOMES
African lady
toned silver print
Zanzibar, ca. 1890
Coll. Civici Musei, Pavia

VITTORIO SELLA
(Italian, 1859–1943)
Nude study
gelatin silver print
Uganda, 1906
Coll. Fondazione Sella e Istituto
di Fotografia Alpina "Vittorio Sella"

Eroticism was associated with the
fascination of that virgin land. It is
impossible to think of the colonial
era—or for that matter of any impe-
rialistic enterprise—without evoking
myths of power, the most ambiguous being perhaps the claim of extreme sexual freedom, which the
Europeans intimately linked with the
conviction of Western racial and
cultural superiority.

(Photographer Unknown)
Masai
gelatin silver print
East Africa. ca. 1900
Coll. Museum für Völkerkunde, Vienna

Many photographers sought to
preserve a record of cultures that
were changing and in some cases
being destroyed by the impact of an
alien civilization and technology.
This was the case of the Masai of
Kenya: herdsmen, aristocrats, warriors, carriers of tall spears, drinkers
of blood and milk, lion-killers. Isak
Dinesen described them as "fighters
who had been stopped from
fighting, a dying lion with his claws
clipped, a castrated nation. Their
weapons have been taken from
them, their big shields even, and in
the Game Reserve the lions follow
their cattle."

LEHNERT AND LANDROCK (German)
The Bridge at Kasr-El-Nile
albumen
Egypt, ca. 1900

Coll. Monas Hierogliphica, Milan

Attributed to LUIGI NARETTI
   (Italian, d. 1922)
Danakil woman
albumen
Eritrea or Somalia, ca. 1880
Coll. Monas Hierogliphica, Milan

Ethnographers quickly recognized in
photography a powerful tool for
their scientific investigations. To
facilitate the comparison and classification of the various "native types"
then being discovered, photographers used stereotyped poses, with
the sitter placed against a neutral
background, sometimes next to a
graduated scale, so as to help in
making precise anthropological
measurements. Such photographs
grouped by racial categories were
fairly typical, as were those showing
Africans in the exercise of their
handicrafts and trades, religious
festivals and games.

MAURO LEDRU (Italian)
Massaua, Italian troops get ready to build a decauville railroad
albumen, from the book *Ricordi di Massaua*, 1885
Eritrea, 1885
Coll. Monas Hierogliphica, Milan

J. A. DA CUNHA MORAES (Portuguese)
Arrival of a Caravan
photogravure
Angola, ca. 1880
Coll. Monas Hierogliphica, Milan

FRANCIS FRITH (British, 1822–98)
Crocodile on a Sand-bank
albumen
Nubia 1858
Coll. Monas Hierogliphica, Milan

"It is very doubtful whether the banks of the Nile present to most travellers any object of greater interest than the monster which we have here depicted. The Crocodile is almost as much one of the wonders of the 'Father of rivers' as temple ruins. I confess that I regard him as an essential ornament to its banks, he is one—almost the only living one—of the venerable 'institutions' of ancient Egypt. How imposing—how grimly magnificent his aspect! His features especially are hideously grand: He has no lips, and his great serrated jaws seem to have no particular line—the sharp white teeth are set therein with a bold irregularity which is charmingly Gothic. His impenetrable hide is glossy and green, marvelously jointed and overlapped; his hands are almost as beautiful and delicate as a lady's." Francis Frith, *Egypt, Sinai and Palestine*.

(Photographer Unknown)
The Africanist
ca. 1900
Coll. Monas Hierogliphica, Milan

This picture summarizes with extraordinary vividness a number of common features of nineteenth-century studio photography. The explorer on his return from Africa is depicted according to people's belief of what explorers should look like; in this case, however, it is likely to have been a mere disguise, since many true explorers had their portraits taken in fancy African or Arab costumes or together with African servants.

A. BARATTI (Italian)
Camel Driver, Bilen Tribe
toned gelatin silver print
ca. 1910
Coll. Monas Hierogliphica, Milan

NOTES

INTRODUCTION

1. V. S. Naipaul, *A Bend in the River,* p. 79.
2. Ibid., p. 17.
3. John Hanning Speke, *Journal of the Discovery of the Source of the Nile,* p. 138.
4. William Gilpin, *Three Essays on Picturesque Beauty or Picturesque Travel,* London, 1808.
5. *Lloyd's Guidebook,* London, 1864.
6. Quoted in Royal Commonwealth Society, *Commonwealth in Focus,* p. 19.
7. Paolo Godio, *Vita Africana,* p. 36.
8. Royal Commonwealth Society, *Commonwealth in Focus,* p. 19.

CHAPTER 1

1. Arthur Rimbaud, *Correspondence,* in *Oeuvres complètes,* Paris, Gallimard, 1972, p. 329.
2. Guy de Maupassant, *Au Soleil,* pp. 10–11.
3. Pierre Loti, *Aziyade,* p. 44.
4. Gustave Flaubert, *Correspondance,* vol. I, pp. 462–3.
5. Pierre Loti, *L'Exilée,* p. 170.

6. Arthur Rimbaud, *Une saison en enfer,* in *Oeuvres complètes,* Paris, Gallimard, 1972, p. 96.
7. Joseph Conrad, *Lord Jim,* p. 272.
8. Loti, *L'Exilée,* p. 170.
9. Paul Valéry, *Regards sur le monde actuel et autres essais,* Paris, Gallimard, 1956, p. 212.
10. Victor Segalen, *Voix mortes, musique maori,* p. 178.
11. Henry Beaufoy, quoted in Hallett, Robbin, *Records of the African Association 1788–1833,* London, 1964, p. 36.
12. Leo Africanus, *History and Description of Africa,* London, 1884.
13. Richard Burton, *The Lake Regions of Central Africa,* p. 60.
14. Speke, *Journal of the Discovery,* p. 95.
15. Speke, *Journal of the Discovery,* p. 129.
16. Samuel Baker, *The Albert Nyanza,* p. 48.
17. Baker, *The Albert Nyanza,* p. 82.
18. David Livingstone, *Narrative of an Expedition to Zambesi and Its Tributaries,* New York, 1866, p. 115.
19. David Livingstone, *The Last Journals of David Livingstone in Central Africa,* London, Horace Walles, 1864, p. 65.
20. Letter of Leopold II to Stanley, 1879, quoted in Stanley, *The Congo and Founding of Its Free State,* New York, 1885, p. 77.

CHAPTER 2

1. Winston Churchill, *The River War*, pp. 18–19.
2. Winston Churchill, *My African Journey*, p. 113.

CHAPTER 3

1. Paul Gauguin, *Lettres de Gauguin*, Paris, Grasset. 1946, p. 80.
2. Eugène Delacroix, "Variations on Beauty," *Revue des Deux Mondes*, July 15, 1857.
3. Isak Dinesen, *Out of Africa*, p. 43.
4. Alfredo Oriani, *La lotta politica in Italia: Origini della lotta attuale, 476–1887*, p. 340.
5. M. Piscicelli, *Nel paese del Bongo-bongo*, p. 35.
6. Guglielmo Massaja, *In Abissinia e tra i Galla*, pp. 103–4.
7. Burton, *The Lake Regions*, p. 64.
8. Baker, *The Albert Nyanza*, p. 49.
9. Mary Kingsley, *Travels in West Africa*, London, 1897, p. 659.
10. Edmondo De Amicis, *Marocco*, p. 138.
11. Pierre Loti, *Maroc*, p. iv.
12. Friedrich Schiller, *Über naive und sentimentalische Dichtung*, pp. 39–40.
13. Harry Johnston, *Uganda Protectorate*, London, Hutchison, 1902, p. 232.
14. Quoted in Royal Commonwealth Society, *Commonwealth in Focus*, p. 9.

CHAPTER 4

1. Denis Diderot, *Supplément au voyage de Bougainville*, Paris. E. Drosz, 1935, p. 90.
2. Luigi Robecchi-Bricchetti, *Nel'Harrar*, p. 42.
3. *Le questioni del Benadir, Atti e relazioni dei Commissari della Società n. Gustavo Chiesi e avv. Ernesto Travelli*, Milan, Stab. Bellini, 1904, pp. 162–3.
4. Rodolfo Graziani, circular letter *Relazioni di ufficiali con donne indigene*, May 17, 1932.
5. *Fama: Rassegna di Scienze, Lettere ed Arti*, March 20, 1840.
6. Charles Baudelaire, "L'Invitation au voyage," *Les Fleurs du mal*, Paris, Gallimard, 1954, p. 127.

CHAPTER 5

1. Schiller, *Über naive und sentimentalische Dichtung*, p. 43.
2. Eugène Delacroix, *Fragments métaphysiques*, September 21, 1854, in *Journal 1822–1863*.

3. Delacroix, *Fragments métaphysiques*, May 1, 1850.
4. Alexander von Humbolt, *Cosmos, Essai d'une description physique du monde*, Milan, Turati, 1846–49.
5. Schiller, *Über naive und sentimentalische Dichtung*, p. 38.
6. Henry M. Stanley, *Through the Dark Continent*, New York, 1878, p. 154.
7. Aldous Huxley, "The Archimedes," in *Little Mexican*, London, 1933, pp. 277–8.
8. H. Rider Haggard, *Allan Quatermain*, p. 14.
9. Haggard, *Allan Quatermain*, p. 19.
10. Francis Frith, *Egypt, Sinai and Palestine*, quote from "Pharaoh's Bed, Philae" caption.
11. Gustave Flaubert, *Notes de voyages*, p. 186.
12. Luigi Barzini, *Sotta la tenda*, p. 116.
13. Joseph Conrad, *Heart of Darkness*, p. 51.
14. Conrad, *Heart of Darkness*, p. 48.

CHAPTER 6

1. Conrad, *Heart of Darkness*, p. 98.
2. Pierre Loti, *La Mort de Philae*, p. 10.
3. Flaubert, *Correspondance*, vol. I, pp. 413–14.
4. Witelo (ca. 1230–1275). Polish philosopher and scientist. Quoted in Venturi, *Storia della critica d'arte*, p. 81, Einaudi, Torino, 1964; English ed. *History of Art Criticism*, New York, 1936, E. P. Dutton & Co.

CHAPTER 7

1. Stanley, *Through the Dark Continent*, p. 189.
2. Stanley, *Through the Dark Continent*, p. 173.
3. Stanley, *Through the Dark Continent*, p. 147.
4. De Amicis, *Memorie*, p. 144.
5. Dinesen, *Out of Africa*, p. 98.
6. Conrad, *Heart of Darkness*, p. 78.
7. De Maupassant, *Au Soleil*, p. 70.
8. Vittorio Bottego, *Il Giuba esplorato*, p. 79.
9. De Maupassant, *Au Soleil*, p. 71.
10. Conrad, *Heart of Darkness*, p. 32.
11. Louis-Ferdinand Céline, *Journey to the End of the Night*, p. 117.
12. *Le Journal des Goncourts*, 23/11/1863.
13. Loti, *Aziyade*, p. 152.
14. Keith and Willward, *L'Oeuvre de Pierre Loti*, p. 12.

THE PHOTOGRAPHERS

The following list is by no means definitive. It represents—among the vast number of photographers whose work I have come across in the course of my research—only the relative few on whom I was able to obtain biographical information. The list should, therefore, be viewed only as a first, tentative step toward the identification and recognition of the leading practitioners of photography in Africa.

ABDULLAH FRÈRES (Armenians)
Commercial, 1862–1900s
The brothers Kevork and Wichen Biraderler began as assistants to a German chemist, Rabach, who established the first photographic studio in Anatolia. When Rabach left Constantinople in 1858, they took over the studio and became, from 1862, official photographers to the court of the Turkish sultans. In order to secure their new prestigious status they converted to Islam and changed their name to Abdullah. They were also active in Egypt beginning in the 1870s.

ALLRIDGE, THOMAS JOSHUA
(British, 1874–1916)
Amateur, Sierra Leone
He arrived in Sierra Leone in 1871, where he occupied several positions for commercial companies and in the government civil service. He witnessed much of the fighting during the Hut Tax War in 1898 and is the author of *The Sherbro and Its Hinterland* (1901) and *A Transformed Colony: Sierra Leone As It Was and As It Is* (1910).

ANNARATONE, CARLO (Italian, d. 1931)
Amateur
He was an army doctor, and went to Eritrea in the early 1890s. He fought in World War I on the Macedonian front in the Italian Expeditionary Corps. After the war he returned to Africa, where he held various political positions in Eritrea and Ethiopia. He wrote several articles and books, the most important of which, *In Abissinia* (1914), relates his role in a 1903 prospecting survey to Lake Tana and is illustrated by 192 of his photographs.

ARNOUX, H. (French)
Commercial, Port Said, Egypt 1860s–1880s
He worked sometimes with Zangaki and produced an *Album du Canal* containing views of the Suez Canal and a portrait of Ferdinand de Lesseps. He photographed the Red Sea and Aden.

ARTZ, SIMON (probably Swiss)
Commercial, Egypt 1880s–1920s
His nephew Ezra Newman bought in about 1935 one of the Cairo branches of Lehnert & Landrock.

DE BANVILLE, AYMARD (French)
Amateur
He served as official photographer for the archaeological expedition of 1863–4 of Egyptologist Emmanuel de Rougé. 155 of his plates were copied in de Rougé's *Album Photographique de la Mission remplie en Egypte* (Paris: L. Samson, 1865). The Societé Française de Photographie selected de Banville's photographs for the Paris Salon in 1865.

BARTHOLDI, FRÉDÉRIC-AUGUSTE (French, 1834–1904)
Amateur
A sculptor and creator of the Statue of Liberty. Bartholdi photographed Egypt while traveling there in 1854.

BARZINI, LUIGI (Italian 1874–1947)
Amateur, Lybia 1911, Morocco 1912
He was a journalist and caricaturist for the *Fanfulla* (1898–1900) and then for the *Corriere della Sera*—the largest Italian newspaper—where he worked for 25 years, while at the same time contributing to the London *Daily Telegraph*. In 1900 he was special correspondent in China during the Boxer Rebellion and there took his first photographs. Barzini was a talented amateur and photographed most of the events he witnessed during his professional life. However, none was ever published by a newspaper. He took photographs of the Russo-Japanese War of 1905; of the Paris-Peking motor race he ran in 1907 with Prince Scipione Borghese; of the Italian-Turkish War of 1911. He was then director of the Italian newspaper *Corriere d'America* in New York and of the *Mattino* in Naples. He contributed to several other papers and magazines and wrote several books. In 1934 he was elected senator.

BAUMANN, OSCAR (Austrian)
Amateur
An explorer in East Africa in 1893, who served from 1895 to 1898 as consul in Zanzibar.

BEATO, ANTONIO (Probably Italian, d. 1903)
Commercial, Luxor, Egypt 1862–1900s

BEATO, FELICE A.
Commercial
Reportedly a naturalized British citizen of Venetian origin. In partnership with James Robertson, chief engraver at the Imperial Mint in Constantinople, he photographed in Malta, Egypt, Palestine and Syria c 1853–56. He documented the aftermath of the Indian Mutiny in 1858 and had a studio in Calcutta in partnership with Shepherd 1858–59; then followed the Anglo-French Campaign in China (1860) and established himself as photographer and general trader in Japan c 1864–74. He photographed the Korean War of 1871 and the Wolseley Nile Expedition of 1884–85. In about 1886 to 1908 he was photographer and general trader in Rangoon, Burma.

BECCARI, ODOARDO (Italian, b. 1843)
Amateur. Ethiopia 1870

BÉCHARD, H. (French)
Commercial, Egypt 1870s–80s
He won a gold medal at the Paris Universal Exposition in 1878, and wrote *L'Egypte et la Nubie,* which was published in 1888.

BEDFORD, FRANCIS (British, 1821–1894)
Amateur
He was commanded by Queen Victoria to tour with H.R.H. the Prince of Wales in the East in 1861. He then published *Egypt, the Holy Land and Syria,* 1862.

BENECKE, E. (French)
Amateur
A banker, he photographed in Egypt, Lebanon, and Syria in the years 1852–53. Four of his calotypes are included in an album published by Blaquart-Évrard.

BENGHIAT, J. & SON
Commercial, Egypt 1870s–1880s and Aden (Hôtel de l'Europe) 1880s–1890s

BONFILS, FÉLIX (1831–1885)
Commercial
Born in St.-Hyppolyte-du-Fort, France. He began his professional career as a bookbinder. He was a member of the French military expedition in Lebanon in 1860. In the early 1860s he moved to Alais and became interested in photography, which

he learned from Abel Niépce. In 1867 he settled permanently in Lebanon, established a studio in Beirut, and soon had branches in Alexandria, Cairo, and Alais. In 1871 he reported to the Société Française de Photographie that since his arrival in the Levant he had produced 15,000 prints and 9,000 stereoscopic views. He mainly used wet-collodion glass-plate negatives and albumen printing paper. He published: *Architecture antique: Égypte, Grèce, Asie Mineure* (1872), *Catalogue des vues photographiques de l'Orient* (1876), and *Souvenirs d'Orient—Album pittoresque des sites, villes et ruines les plus remarquables de l'Égypte et de la Nubie, de la Palestine, de la Syrie et de la Grèce* (in 4 volumes, 1877–78). He returned to France periodically and died in 1885 at Alais. His wife, Lydie, and his son Adrien were both photographers working in the family business, but there are strong indications that only Félix traveled to Egypt and photographed there.

BOTTEGO, VITTORIO (Italian, 1860–1897)
Amateur
He was an artillery captain stationed in Eritrea in 1887 and commanded a battery of native troops. He explored the coast of Dancalia in 1891–92 and published a report, *Il Giuba esplorato* (1895), containing 143 etchings mostly copied from his photographs. During a second expedition, while returning to Eritrea after more than 18 months of travel in the Lakes region, he was ambushed and killed with almost all of his companions by a war party of Ethiopians.

BRAGGE, JAMES (British, 1833–1908)
Commercial, South Africa
An apprentice cabinetmaker, he emigrated to South Africa in the early 1860s where he started a photographic business. In the mid-1860s he went to New Zealand, where he continued his trade in Wellington and Auckland.

BRUTON, JAMES EDWARD (British, 1838–1918)
Commercial, South Africa
He was born in Port Elizabeth of 1820 settler parents, and from 1858 to 1874 had photographic studios first in Port Elizabeth and then in Cape Town. In the 1890s he moved to Douglas, on the Isle of Man.

BUCHTA, RICHARD
Amateur, Sudan, Uganda, Congo, about 1880
Published an album of original photographs *Die oberen Nil-Länder* (Berlin: J. F. Stiehm, 1881).

CAMMAS, HENRY (French)
He photographed Egypt in the early 1860s and is the author of a book with André Lefèvre, *La Valée du Nil: Impressions et photographies* (Paris: Hachette, 1862) containing small prints of his work.

CITERNI, CARLO (Italian, 1873–1918)
Amateur
Born in Scarlino, Grosseto
He was an infantry second lieutenant, and was official photographer in the second of Bottego's expeditions. After Bottego was killed he was held prisoner for four months by the Ethiopians; he later told the story of his incarceration in his book *L'Omo* (1899). In 1910–11 he explored southern Somalia and reported his experience in *Ai confini meridionali dell'Etiopia* and *Come si viaggia in Africa* (1914). These publications contain reproductions of his photographs. In the last book, he gave extensive practical advice to those intending to take pictures in Africa.

COMERIO, LUCA (Italian, 1878–1940)
Commercial, 1894–1930s
Born in Milan. He was a photojournalist and cameraman of extraordinary skill, documenting for thirty years the most important historical events in Italy. He began to photograph in 1894, but, as early as 1898 he became involved with moving pictures. In 1909 he owned the largest European film studio. He was a daring cameraman during the war in Libya in 1911 and throughout World War I, producing more than fifty newsreels and thousands of photographs.

COMINI, ALESSANDRO (Italian)
Commercial, Asmara, Eritrea 1900s–1910s
Official photographer of the colony.
He received a silver medal at the Milan Exposition in 1906 and a gold medal at the Turin Exposition in 1911.

COUTINHO, BROTHERS
Commercial, Zanzibar and East Africa
Studio in Zanzibar and Dar-es-Salaam. Had a brief partnership with Gomes in the 1890s.

DA COSTA, GEORGE S. A. (African, b. 1853)
Commercial, Nigeria
He was born in Lagos and educated at the local C.M.S. Training Institution. He was a manager of the C.M.S. Bookshop (1877–1895), and then photographer "after the expenditure of some £30 for special training in all phases of the art." He was the official photographer of the railway construction to Jebba and later to Kaduna. His views are reproduced in Colonial Office publications and some of his landscape and portrait photography can be seen in *The Red Book of West Africa*.

DA SILVA, B. M. A.
Commercial, Lagos, Nigeria, 1910s

DE CLERCQ, LOUIS (French, 1836–1901)
Amateur photographer and archaeologist
He was only 23 years old when he worked on Guillaume Rey's scientific expedition in Syria. There he took a great number of calotypes, many of which he reproduced in a monumental six-volume work he published at his own expense: *Voyage en Orient, 1859–1860, villes, monuments et vues pittoresques, recueil photographique exécuté par Louis De Clercq*, containing more than 200 images of the Holy Land, Egypt (41 prints in the fifth volume), and Spain. He went to Syria again in the years 1862, 1863, and 1893, collecting oriental antiquities that his family donated to the Musée du Louvre after his death.

DE LORD, A. R. P.
Commercial, Zanzibar 1890s

DE SIMONI, GIOVANNI (Italian)
Amateur, Egypt, Algeria, Tunisia, and Eritrea 1900s

DIAS, E. C.
Commercial, Zanzibar 1890s

DU CAMP, MAXIME (French, 1822–1894)
Amateur
He was born in Paris, to a wealthy family, and always had the means and connections to live as he liked. Fond of history, archaeology and travels, he had already visited Greece, Turkey, and Algeria, when in 1849 he persuaded the French Ministry of Public Instruction to assign him an archaeological mission in the Middle East. He took along a number of cameras in an effort to document the Pharaonic and Arab monuments.

He took lessons in photography from Gustave Le Gray and, together with his close friend Gustave Flaubert, who was supposed to record in writing the expedition's achievements, he visited, in the years 1849–51, Egypt, Nubia, Palestine, and Syria. After twenty-one months Du Camp had made 220 calotypes and returned to France, where he published a successful photographic album, which was brought out in twenty-five weekly installments of five plates each, at a price of 500 gold francs for the whole set. He gave an account of his photographic experience in his *Souvenirs littéraires,* but soon left photography for good in order to write novels, poetry, historical essays, and literary criticism. He co-founded the *Revue de Paris.* He died in Baden-Baden.

DUMAS, TANCREDE R. (French, d. 1905)
Commercial
Studio in Beirut. He photographed the Holy Land and Egypt, 1860s–1870s.

FERRANDI, UGO (Italian, 1852–1928)
Amateur
Born in Novara. From 1885 on he took part in several exploration expeditions in Somalia and founded the trading post and fort of Lugh in 1895, which greatly contributed to stabilization of the occupation of the colony. He held top positions in the Italian colonial service and wrote *Lugh* (1903), a book illustrated by his photographs, on the ethnological, geographical, and economic characteristics of Somalia. He died in Novara.

FERREIRA, JOSÉ HONORATO
Commercial. Cabo Verde and Loanda, Angola, 1910s

FIORILLO, F.
Commercial, Egypt
He took photographs of Aswan Dam construction in the early 1900s.

FIORILLO, LUIGI (Italian)
Commercial. Alexandria, Egypt 1870s–1890s
His *cartes de visite* were praised in *Murray's Handbook for Egypt* (1875); he specialized in views and ethnic portraits from Palestine, Egypt, Ethiopia, and Algeria. He documented the Egyptian army rebellion of 1881 led by Arabi Pasha against the Anglo-French Condominium administering Egypt and the ten-hour bombardment of Alexandria on July 11, 1882. Fiorillo afterward issued a volume of photographs entitled *Album souvenir d'Alexandrie: Ruines,* a grim record of the havoc wreaked by the bombardment. In 1887, as a guest of the artillery captain Count Carlo Michelini, he produced a photographic report of the Italian military campaign in Abyssinia. He won numerous medals and prizes in the Exhibitions of Naples (1871), Paris (1878), Boston and Ottawa (1885).

FLANDRIN (French)
Commercial, Casablanca, Morocco 1910s–1950s

FRITH, FRANCIS (British, 1822–1898)
He was born in Chesterfield, Derbyshire, and attended Ackworth School and Quaker Camp Hill School, ca. 1828–34. He left school at sixteen and was apprenticed to a Sheffield cutlery firm (1838–43). He started a wholesale grocery trade in Liverpool, cornered the Greek raisin crop (1845–56) and became rich. In 1850 he bought a partnership in a printing firm and began taking photographs. In 1853 he was one of the seven founding members of the Liverpool Photographic Society. He went to Egypt in 1856, to Egypt and Palestine in 1857–58; a third time, in 1859–60, he went 1,500 miles up the Nile, past the Second Cataract. His Middle East photographs were published in eleven books and three sets of stereos. In 1859 he moved his printing firm (Frith & Co.) to Reigate, added a photographic printing department, and was active until about 1885. He died at Reigate.

FRY, WILLIAM ELLERTON (British, 1846–1930)
Amateur, Rhodesia
Fry arrived in South Africa in 1872, where he worked as a farmer, trader, prospector; he was then secretary and computer at the Royal Observatory in Cape Town, where, in 1890, he became assistant astronomer royal. He was part of the Mashonaland Pioneer Column in 1890 as assistant to Selous, intelligence officer, meteorologist, and official photographer. Later he worked on the Salisbury–Tete telegraph and traveled in Australia and New Zealand.

GEDGE, ERNEST (British, 1862–1935)
Amateur, East Africa
After some time spent in India, he was the *Times* correspondent in Uganda and Mashonaland (1892–93). After a short stay in the Yukon prospecting for mineral resources (1898–99), he returned to Africa and was in Rhodesia in 1900 and elsewhere in East Africa in 1902–5. He then moved to the Far East.

GIRAULT DE PRANGEY, JOSEPH-PHILIBERT (French, 1804–1892)
Amateur
He was born in Langres, Burgundy, and was a landowner and expert in Arab history and architecture. He became a founder in 1834 of the Langres Archaeological Society and in 1838 of the Langres Antiquity Museum. He learned the daguerreotype process in 1841 and traveled through Italy, Syria, Palestine, the Middle East, and Greece in 1842–44, bringing back to Langres more than a thousand daguerreotypes of an unusually large format. He never left Langres again. He is the author of *Monuments arabes et moresques de Cordove, Séville et Grenade* (1836), *Essai sur l'architecture des Arabes et des Mores en Espagne, en Sicile et en Barbarie* (1841), and *Monuments arabes d'Égypte, de Syrie et d'Asie Mineure* (1846). In this last book some of his photographic work was reproduced as engravings.

GOMES, A. C. & SON
Commercial, Zanzibar
The firm was founded in about 1868 and had a brief partnership with J. B. Coutinho in the mid-1890s. Business was continued by P. F. Gomes (d. 1932), and a branch was opened in Dar es Salaam in the 1930s.

GRANT, JAMES AUGUSTUS (British, 1827–1892)
Amateur, East Africa
After serving in India as an officer in the Bengal army (1846–68), he accompanied Speke in his expedition to the source of the

Nile (1860–63). He tried photography at the beginning of the expedition, but soon abandoned it in favor of sketching. He also served as an intelligence officer during the Abyssinian Campaign of 1867–68.

GRAY BROTHERS
Commercial, Kimberley, South Africa 1870s

GREENE, JOHN B. (American, 1833–1857)
Greene was an amateur archaeologist and founding member of the Société Française de Photographie. He traveled to Algeria and, in 1852, to Egypt, where he participated in the excavation of Medinet Habou in Thebes. On his return to France he published an album *Le Nil. Monuments. Paysages. Explorations photographiques,* containing 94 prints from wax-paper negatives and a number of scientific papers. He died in Paris at the age of 24.

GREGSON, FRANCIS (British)
Amateur
War correspondent during the Sudan campaign in 1898.

GROS, H. F.
Commercial, Transvaal (South Africa)
Of Swiss origin, he came to South Africa in the late 1860s. He opened studios in Bloemfontein and Kimberley in the early 1870s, toured Pilgrim's Rest goldfields in 1874–75, and finally settled down in Pretoria, till 1895, when he returned to Europe. He documented several aspects of the first Boer War. He also published an illustrated book: *Picturesque aspects of the Transvaal.*

HAMMERSCHMIDT, W. (German)
Commercial
Egypt and Middle East 1850s–1860s

HARRIS, ROBERT
Commercial, Port Elizabeth, South Africa, c. 1880–94
He produced several illustrated books: *Photographic views of Port Elizabeth and Neighbourhood* (c. 1876), *Southampton to South Africa* (by Charles Cowen with photographs by Harris, 1882), *Photographic Album of South African Scenery* (1880s), *South Africa Illustrated* (1888).

HATTERSLEY, CHARLES WILLIAM (British, 1866–1934)
Amateur, Uganda
C.M.S. missionary in Uganda from 1897 and author of *Uganda by the Pen and the Camera* (1906), *The Baganda at Home* (1908), *Erastus, Slave and Prince* (1910).

HAWES, ALBERT GEORGE SIDNEY (British, d. 1897)
Amateur, Nyasaland
After serving ten years in the Royal Marines (1859–69) and in Japan (1871–84), Hawes was promoted "consul for the territories of the African Kings and Chiefs in the districts adjacent to Lake Nyasa" (1885–87) and was then on special duty in Zanzibar (1888–89). He later held various consular offices in the South Seas Islands.

HILY, L.
Commercial, Lourenço Marques and Beira, Mozambique 1900s–1910s

HOLM, J. C. A. (African, b. 1888)
Commercial, Nigeria and Ghana
Holm left school at the age of eighteen and became a partner in the photographic business of his father, N. Walwin Holm. While his father was in England, he managed the studio, and in 1919 he reopened a branch in Accra (High Street).

HOLM, N. WALWIN (African, b. 1865)
Commercial, Ghana and Nigeria
Holm was born and educated in Accra. At the age of seventeen he became a commercial photographer. He moved to Lagos in 1896. In 1897 he was the first photographer of the colony to be enrolled as a member of the Royal Photographic Society of Great Britain. He won the first and second prizes at the Agricultural Show at Sekondi in 1907. Many of his photographs illustrate the Nigerian section of *The Red Book of West Africa.* In 1910 he went to England for his health and studied law, and in 1917 he returned to Lagos to practice as a barrister.

IRANIAN, M. (Probably Armenian)
Commercial, Egypt 1880s

ITIER, JULES (French, 1802–1877)
Amateur, Egypt 1845

KIRK, SIR JOHN (British)
A member of Livingstone's Zambesi expedition in 1858. During the journey he experimented with several photographic processes, including waxed paper (a variation of Fox Talbot's paper negative-positive process), Hill Norton's dry collodion, and ordinary wet collodion.

LANGAKI
Commercial, Egypt 1880s

LAZARUS, J. & M. (probably British)
Commercial, Studios in Lisbon, Portugal and Lourenço Marques, Mozambique c. 1900–1910
Lazarus photographed throughout Portuguese East Africa, Kenya, and Rhodesia and published albums in photogravure.

LEDRU, FILIPPO (Italian)
Commercial
He was one of the earliest Italian photoreporters; he documented the Casamicciola earthquake in 1883, the cholera epidemic in Messina, and the great Etna eruption in 1887. He went to Africa three times to document the first Italian colonial experience. He landed with the first Italian troops in Massawa in 1885; on his third trip in 1896, all of his cameras were lost in the battle of Adwa.

LEHNERT & LANDROCK
 LEHNERT, RUDOLF (Austrian)
 LANDROCK, ERNST (German, ca. 1885–1968)
Commercial
Lehnert and Landrock were friends making their traditional Grand Tour when they decided to open a photographic studio in Tunis in 1904. Because of their nationality, at the outbreak of World War I, the studio was confiscated. At the end of the war they regained their plates and, in 1919, founded in Leipzig the Orient Kunst Verlag. In 1922 Lehnert traveled throughout the Middle East with an assistant and in 1924 opened with Landrock a studio in Cairo. The partnership was dissolved in 1927, when Lehnert left Cairo to open a new studio in Tunis. In Cairo "Lehnert & Landrock, Ernst Landrock succ." gradu-

ally became a bookstore and a postcard publisher and was sold in 1938 to Landrock's son-in-law.

LEKEGIAN, G. (Probably Armenian)
Commercial, Egypt 1860s–1900s
Holder of the official title "Photographer to the British Army of Occupation."

LENOX, AMBROSE
Commercial, Molteno, South Africa 1890s
Lenox was a chemist who set up a pharmacy and a photographic studio in 1894 and photographed everything of interest in and around town; 1,400 of his glass plates still survive.

LEOMY, DIONYSIUS
Commercial, Freetown, Sierra Leone 1890s

LEREBOURS, N. P. (French)
Some of the engravings published in the *Excursions Daguerriennes* (1841–3) were copied from his photographs of Egypt.

LISK-CAREW BROTHERS, ALPHONSO
 AND ARTHUR (Africans)
Commercial, Freetown, Sierra Leone
Active 1905–1920s
"The firm are clever exponents of photography in all its branches, and have the distinction of the use of the Royal coat of arms, as they were appointed photographers to H. R. H. the Duke of Connaught.
 There is probably no establishment in Freetown that is visited by more passengers from the steamers than that of Messrs. Lisk-Carew Bros. The reason of its popularity is because of the extensive stock of postcard views of Freetown and Sierra Leone, as well as because of its large assortment of fancy goods, stationery, and photographic requisites." Quoted from Allister MacMillan, *The Red Book of West Africa*, 1920.

LLOYD, JAMES
Commercial, Durban, South Africa c. 1875–88

LOBO, ALFRED
Commercial, Entebbe, Uganda 1900s–1920s
Possibly previously employed in the Locomotive Department of Uganda Railway.

LORENT, AUGUST JACOB
Commercial
He had a studio in Venice in 1853–55, but worked also in Spain, Algeria, and Egypt. His photographs were awarded a prize at the Paris Universal Exposition of 1855.

LUTTERODT, F. R. C. (African, b. 1871)
Commercial, West Africa
Born in Accra, Gold Coast Colony (Ghana). After spending a year as clerk in the Audit Department of the Government Service, he started business in Accra as a photographer in 1889. Active in the 1890s at Victoria, in the Cameroons, in French Gabon, Fernando Po, San Thome and Prince's Island. He re-opened in Accra in 1900. He was appointed to accompany the Governor during the visit of the latter to Togoland in 1919 and through the Western Province, Ashanti, Northern Territories and the Eastern Province in 1920.

MACKINDER, HALFORD (British)
Amateur
Explorer, geographer and mountain climber, he was the first to conquer the summit of Mount Kenya on September 12, 1899, and documented the expedition with his Kodak camera. Later he entered the civil service and eventually became a Member of the British Parliament.

MANTEGAZZA, VICO (Italian)
Illustrazione Italiana special correspondent in Eritrea c. 1885

MARIETTE-BEY, AUGUSTE (French, 1821–1851)
Published his photographs as photogravures in 1878 in the two volumes *Voyage dans la Haute-Égypte.*

MAUNIER, V. G. (French)
He was a photographer from Paris who in 1854 was commissioned by the Egyptian Viceroy to reproduce photographically the Pharaonic monuments. Some of his pictures were printed, probably in album form, in Lille by Blanquart-Evrard in 1854–5. He remained in Egypt, where he owned for a brief time a pawnshop, and he traded Egyptian antiquities for twenty years. He was an amateur archaeologist of some talent and helped Mariette in his Luxor excavations. In 1863 he became administrator for a wealthy Egyptian landowner; he returned to France a rich man and made many large donations to the Louvre.

MEE, J. R.
Commercial, South Africa
Studios in Durban 1880, Cathcart 1884, Kimberley 1889–91, Wynberg 1891

MICHEL, CHARLES
Ethiopia 1897–98

MIDDLEBROOK, J. E.
Commercial, South Africa
He had studios in Kimberley 1888–94 and in Durban 1898–99.

MORAES, J. A. DA CUNHA (Portuguese)
Commercial. Studio in Loanda, Angola ca. 1863–89
He traveled extensively throughout the colony, San Thome Island, and Cabinda/Portuguese Congo. He published in four volumes *Africa Occidental* (1885–87), illustrated with several hundred photogravures and a number of photographic albums on the Portuguese colony of Angola. He won awards at the expositions of Rio de Janeiro (1876), Paris (1878), and Porto (1878 and 1882). Most probably his was a family business, since various signatures appear on very similar photographs (C. Moraes, A. C. C. Moraes, and Irmaos).

MURRAY, JOHN H. (British)
Commercial, South Africa 1880s–90s
He was a familiar figure touring Natal in a horse-drawn trap, taking his darkroom with him and doing all of his developing on the spot. His photographs were exhibited at the London Colonial Exhibition in 1886.

NARETTI, LUIGI (Italian, d. 1922)
Commercial, Eritrea c. 1889–1920s
Born in Parella, Ivrea. He came to Eritrea in the late 1880s, where his cousin Giacomo, a craftsman appointed to the court of King Johannes of Abyssinia, had lived since the 1860s. He initially established a studio in Massawa, but soon moved to Asmara. For more than thirty years he documented the history of the colony and painted a photographic portrait of the people and places of Eritrea and Tigrai. He died in Asmara.

NEGRETTI & ZAMBRA
Commercial, Photographers? and publishers
of stereo series, London
China and Japan 1850s–60s and South Africa 1870s–80s

NICOTRA, F. AND G. (Italians)
Commercial, Eritrea 1890s
The two Nicotra brothers, together with Ledru, bought in the 1870s the studio of the French photographer Jacques, in Messina (Sicily). However, their association with Ledru did not last long, and in 1881 it ended. Their photographic works (mostly landscapes and series on typical costumes of Sicily and Calabria) were successful, and soon they were able to open branches in Acireale and, in the 1890s, in Massawa, Eritrea. F. Nicotra was in charge of this African branch and documented the first Italian colonial wars as well as local customs and scenery.

NORMAND, ALFRED NICOLAS (French, 1822–1909)
Amateur, Tunisia and Egypt 1890s
The son of the Architect Louis-Eléonor Normand, Alfred attended the Ecole des Beaux-Arts in Paris, specializing in architecture. In 1846 he won the Rome Grand Prize and settled in Rome, where in 1851 he began taking photographs. The same year he met Du Camp and Flaubert on their way back from the East and took their portraits. He then traveled through southern Italy and Greece and the following year went to Constantinople. From 1852 he worked as an architect and inspector of public works for the City of Paris. For more than thirty years he abandoned photography. In 1885 he started photographing again and in a few years his archive totaled 3,500 plates, mostly on architectural subjects. While he photographed mostly in the French provinces, 400 plates document his numerous trips in Italy, Tunisia, Egypt, the Ottoman empire, Russia, and northern Europe.

OLDENBURG, RUDOLF (Austrian, d. 1932?)
Amateur, Cameroon and Guinea
Born in Vienna, he lived in Conakry for many years, where he was a merchant and factor for a Bremen firm. From about 1907 to 1913 he administered the German Cameroon Society. At the outbreak of the First World War he returned to Austria and died in Vienna.

PEREIRA, MANUEL (Portuguese)
Commercial, Ianga, German Oriental Africa 1880s and Mozambique 1890s where he was the government's official photographer.

PERIDIS
Commercial, Cairo, Egypt 1880s

PÖCH, RUDOLF (Austrian, 1870–1921)
Amateur
Born in Tarnopol, and studied in Vienna where he became a doctor. In 1896 he traveled and studied extensively, taking photographs of the countries he visited: Egypt and India (1897), New Guinea and Australia (1904–6), and South Africa, Botswana, Zimbabwe, and Namibia (1907). He received a Ph.D. in Munich and, from 1910, taught anthropology and ethnology at the University of Vienna.

POTTECHER, FERNAND
Commercial, Rabat, Morocco 1910s–1960s

POWELL-COTTON, GORDON (British)
Ethiopia 1899–1900

RAVENSCROFT, THOMAS DANIEL
Hermanus Cape, South Africa, 1880s–1950s
He depicted the towns of the Western Cape and some leading personalities; in the 1880s he was employed by the Cape Colonial Government to produce photographs of the railway system for publicity purposes.

ROBECCHI-BRICCHETTI, LUIGI (Italian, 1855–1926)
Amateur
Born in Pavia. He graduated in engineering from the Zurich Polytechnic School and studied foreign languages in Karlsruhe. He also was a lover of magic and fond of prestidigitation, a skill he often used during his travels. In 1887, while making a business trip in Egypt, he went to the ancient oasis of Jupiter Ammonius. During this expedition, as in the following ones, he brought with him a camera. In four successive expeditions (1888, 1890, 1891, and 1903) he visited much of Somalia. He was a talented amateur in botany, zoology (he discovered 67

new species), mineralogy, agronomics, meteorology, oceanography, and topography. He was the author of more than 45 publications, some of which are illustrated by his photographs. He died in Pavia.

ROWLANDS, DR. JOHN WILLIAM C. M. G.
(British, 1852–1925)
Amateur, Lagos, Nigeria
Served as a surgeon in India (1877–8) and then in the Lagos Colony (1880–97). He compiled an album of Lagos views in 1885.

ROYAL ENGINEERS
Since the Crimean War the rudiments of photography had been taught to some sappers, but a series of mishaps frustrated this first attempt and not until 1856 was a photographic section formed as part of the Telegraph School at Chatham; a separate School of Photography was formed in 1874. Important photographic work includes the recording of the Abyssinian Campaign of 1867–68 and the Suakin Campaign in 1885 (in Sudan against the Mahdist forces).

SALINA, VITTORIO (Italian)
Tripoli, Libya 1911

SANGIOVANNI, EZIO (Italian)
Photographer of the battle of Adwa (1896)

SAVOIA, LUIGI AMEDEO Duca degli Abruzzi
(Italian, 1873–1933)
Amateur
Born in Madrid, he was the third son of Prince Amedeo, Duca d'Aosta, kinsman of the Italian royal family. From his youth he was keen on geographical expeditions and mountain-climbing. After climbing several of the highest peaks in the Alps, he organized geographical expeditions that made him world-famous: Mount Saint Elia in Alaska (1897), toward the Pole North (1899), the Ruwenzori in Uganda (1906), the Karakorum in India (1909). He fought in World War I on the Italian front. Shortly after the war he left Italy to live in Somalia, where he devoted himself to the agricultural development of the colony and completed the exploration of River Uebi Scebeli. He used photography, and later film, to document his deeds. Vittorio Sella and his assistant Erminio Botta accompanied him in Alaska, in Africa, and in the Karakorum. He died in Somalia in the Scidli region.

SCHOELLER, MAX (Austrian)
Amateur. Tanzania 1896–97

SÉBAH, J. PASCAL (Turkish?, d. 1890)
Commercial
He opened a studio in Constantinople in 1868, where he worked with Joailler, and in Cairo.

SELLA, VITTORIO (Italian, 1859–1943)
Born in Biella, he studied chemistry, optics, and mechanics. His uncle, Quintino Sella, Italian minister of finance and founder of the Italian Alpine Club, introduced him to mountaineering. His father, Giuseppe Venanzio Sella, author in 1853 of *Il Plico del fotografo,* the first treatise on photography ever written by an Italian, conveyed to him his passion for photography. Using the wet calotype process he took his first photographs in 1879 from the summit of Mount Mars. From 1881 onward he used the gelatin silver process exclusively and from 1882 to 1892 he took pictures of the whole Alps range using 30 × 40 cm. glass plates. From 1893 he started using lighter cameras, easier to employ in difficult conditions. He participated in three mountain-climbing expeditions in the Caucasus in 1889, 1890, and 1896; he climbed with Freshfield the Kangchenjunga in the Himalayas (1899) and, with the Duca degli Abruzzi, Mount Saint Elia in Alaska (1897), Mount Ruwenzori in Uganda (1906), and the Karakorum in Tibet (1909).

SIKORA, F.
Commercial, Madagascar and Reunion 1890s

SILVEIRA, J. (Portuguese)
Commercial. Luanda, Angola, c. 1872–78
The photographer J. A. de Silveira, who worked in Hong Kong (1866–67), might be the same person. Silveira's plate archive was probably bought by Moraes.

SILVESTRI, MICHELE (Italian, 1849–1936)
Commercial, Eritrea 1896–1936
Born in Roccaraso. He went to Eritrea to report the 1896 war, but then decided to stay there and established a studio in Asmara. He died in Asmara.

SMITH, JOHN SHAW (Irish, 1811–1874)
Amateur
Smith was a landowner in County Cork and traveled throughout Europe, the Near and Middle East in 1850–52, taking almost 300 photographs by the waxed paper and calotype processes. He was one of the first Europeans to photograph the cave city of Petra. He died in Dublin.

STHULMANN, FRANZ (German)
Amateur, East Africa
As a naturalist, he took part in Emin Pasha's expedition to the equatorial lakes (1890–1) and was the first to attempt the ascent of Mount Ruwenzori. He took pictures of the expedition's progress, some of which are reproduced in his book *Mit Emin Pasha ins Herz von Africa,* 1894.

TEYNARD, FÉLIX (French, 1817–1892)
Amateur
An engineer born in Grenoble, Savoy, who went to Egypt in 1851–52 and 1869. 160 of his photographs were included in the book *Égypte et Nubie. Sites et monuments les plus intéressants pour l'étude de l'art et de l'histoire. Atlas photographique accompagné de plans et d'une table explicative servant de complément á la grande "Description d'Égypte."* Published by Goupil in two volumes in 1853 and 1858, the book cost the incredible sum of nearly 1,000 francs.

TRAVERSI, LEOPOLDO (Italian, b. 1856)
Amateur and explorer
Born in Piacastagnaio, Siena. An intelligence and political officer for the Italian government, Traversi made frequent trips to Abyssinia. He was the author of several scientific reports on the geography and the people of that country. *I miei trentacinque anni di missione nell'Alta Etiopia* (1885–95) by Cardinal Guglielmo Massaja is illustrated by a great number of his photographs of African life.

TUMINELLO, LUDOVICO (Italian, 1824–1907)
Commercial
He was born in Rome, and worked there until 1842. He was forced into exile for his participation in the 1848 uprisings. The same year he established a photographic business in Turin, but in 1870 returned to Rome and the following year documented the siege and fall of the city at the hands of the

Piedmontese army. He then became official photographer to the Pope, succeeding D'Alessandri. In 1870 he documented the African expedition in Eritrea of Marchese Orazio Antinori. His work was exhibited in Turin in 1858, in Florence in 1870, in Vienna in 1873, and in Paris in 1878. He closed his business in 1903, and his plates were auctioned off and dispersed. He died in Rome.

TURTON, W. S. (British)
Amateur, Lagos, Nigeria
He worked there for the Public Works Department (1891–4) and, as a photographer, he accompanied Sir Gilbert Carter's Lagos Interior Expedition in 1893.

VERNET, HORACE (French, 1789–1863)
Amateur, Egypt 1839
His was the first recorded photograph of Africa. In 1842 he accompanied the French army to Algeria and later traveled in Russia and in the Middle East. His Orientalist works were immensely successful and he was particularly famous for his battle paintings.

WHEELHOUSE, C. G. (British)
Amateur
Wheelhouse was the medical officer of a yachting party of English gentlemen visiting the Middle East and Egypt in 1849–50, and he photographed the places visited, putting them together in an album, which he titled *Photographic Sketches from the Shores of the Mediterranean.*

XIMENES, EDOARDO (Italian, 1852–1932)
He was born in Sicily, and studied art and particularly painting in Naples, but then felt attracted by journalism. He moved to Milan, where he became co-founder, with Emilio Treves, and art director of the *Illustrazione Italiana,* which was for fifty years the most prestigious and widely circulated Italian illustrated magazine. He was often special correspondent for his magazine and illustrated his articles and books with his own photographs and sketches. From February to August 1896 he directed the illustrated gazette *La guerra Italo-Abissinia* (*The war between Italy and Abyssinia*); in March 1896 he went to Eritrea to give a firsthand report of the military campaign, and his photographs and pictures are still the best-known iconography of that war. As a painter and sculptor he

participated in several international expositions. In the 1920s he left the *Illustrazione* and Milan, lived for some time in Tripoli, Libya, and then settled in Rome, where he continued working as a journalist.

YOUNG, WILLIAM D. (British)
Commercial, India and East Africa
He came to Africa in the late 1890s after working as a railways photographer in eastern India. He opened a studio in Mombasa (ca. 1899–1904) and then in Nairobi (1905–ca. 1919). He was the "official" freelance photographer of the construction of the Uganda Railway (1896–1903). In the 1920s he became manager of the Swift Press in Nairobi.

ZANGAKI (Turkish?)
Commercial, Port Said, Egypt, 1860s–1880s
He took photographs of Egypt, the Sudan, and the Red Sea coast. He sometimes worked with Arnoux. In the 1870s Bonfils bought some of Zangaki's plates and sold them after having scratched out Zangaki's name and put his own in instead.

BIBLIOGRAPHY

Acerbi, Libero, *Dal Congo al Nilo Azzurro*, Viadana, Portanuova, 1975

Baines, Thomas, "Scenes of South African Travel," in *Illustrated London News*, 1865

Baker, Sir Samuel White, *The Albert Nyanza, Great Basin of the Nile, and Explorations of the Nile Sources*, London, MacMillan, 1866

Barzini, Luigi, *Sotta la tenda*, Piacenza, Rinfreschi, 1915

Beard, Peter H., *The End of the Game*, New York, Doubleday, 1965

Benoit, Pierre, *L'Atlantide*, Paris, Albin Michel, 1949

Bensusan, A. D., *Photography in South Africa*, Fact Paper no. 55, State Information Office, Pretoria, 1958

Bernartz, Johann Martin, *Bilder aus Aethiopien*, Hamburg, 1854

Bertrand, Louis, *Le mirage oriental*, Paris, Perrin, 1910

Birkenhead, F. W. F. S., *Rudyard Kipling*, New York, Random House, 1978

Bottego, Vittorio, *Il Giuba esplorato*, Rome, Loescher, 1895

Bull, Marjorie, and Denfield, Joseph, *Secure the Shadow. The Story of Cape Photography from Its Beginnings to the End of 1870*, Cape Town, 1970

Burton, Sir Richard, *The Lake Regions of Central Africa*, London, 1902

Céline, Louis-Ferdinand, *Journey to the End of the Night*, New York, New Directions, 1959

Churchill, Winston Spencer, *My African Journey*, London, 1908

Churchill, Winston Spencer, *The River War*, Longmans Green, London, 1902

Caillié, René, *Journal d'un voyage à Tembouctou et à Jenné . . .*, Paris, Atlas, 1800

Citerni, Carlo, *Come si viaggia in Africa*, Rome, Tip. dell'Unione, 1913

Cockney, *Trip to the Great Sahara with a Camera*, London, 1906

Conrad, Joseph, *Heart of Darkness*, New York, Penguin Books, 1980

Conrad, Joseph, *Lord Jim*, New York, New American Library, 1961

De Amicis, Edmondo, *Marocco*, Milan, Treves, 1889

De Amicis, Edmondo, *Memorie*, Milan, Treves, 1900

De Amicis, Edmondo, *Poesie*, Milan, Treves, 1881

Delacroix, Eugène, *Journal 1822–1863; Voyage au Maroc 1832*, Paris, Plon, 1960

Denon, Dominique Vivant, *Planches du voyage dans la Haute et la Basse Egypte*, Paris, 1802

Dinesen, Isak (Karen Blixen), *Out of Africa*, New York, Random House, 1972

Bibliography

Flaubert, Gustave, *Correspondance*, Paris, Louis Conard, 1910

Flaubert, Gustave, *Notes de voyages*, Paris, Louis Conard, 1910

Frith, Francis, *Egypt, Sinai and Palestine, Supplementary Volume*, London, William Mackenzie, 1858

Gandolfi, Tertulliano, *I misteri dell'Africa italiana*, 1910

Gau, Franz Christian, *Antiquités de la Nubie*, Paris, 1822

Gianella, Aristide M., *Medaglioni di viaggiatori italiani: Gustavo Bianchi*, in *Per terra e per mare*, 1904, vol. 2, no. 7

Gianella, Aristide M., *Medaglioni di viaggiatori italiani: Giacomo Bove*, in *Per terra e per mare*, 1904, vol. 2, no. 9

Gilpin, William, *Three Essays on Picturesque Beauty and Picturesque Travel*, 1808

Godio, Paolo, *Vita africana; Ricordi d'un viaggio nel Sudan orientale*, Milano, Vallardi, 1885

Goetzmann, William H., *Exploration and Empire*, New York, W. W. Norton, 1978

Grogan, Edward Scott, and Sharp, Arthur H., *Cape to Cairo*, London, 1900

Haggard, H. Rider, *Allan Quatermain*, Leipzig, B. Tauchnitz, 1887

Haggard, H. Rider, *King Solomon's Mines*, Leipzig, B. Tauchnitz, 1886

von Harnier, Wilhem, *Raise an den obern Nil*, Darmstadt und Leipzig, 1866

Huxley, Aldous, *Eyeless in Gaza*, New York, Harper and Row, 1974

Kane, Cheikh Manidou, *L'aventure ambigue*, Paris, 1961 tr., *Ambiguous Adventure*, New York, Walker & Co., 1963

Keith G., and Millward M. A., *L'oeuvre de Pierre Loti et l'esprit fin du siècle*, Paris, Millet, 1955

Kipling, Rudyard, *Something of Me*. Italian trans. *Qualcosa di me*, Turin, Einaudi, 1986

Krapf, Johann Ludwig, *Travels, Researches and Missionary Labours during 18 Years' Residence in Eastern Africa Together with Journeys to Jagga, Usambara, Ukambani, Shoa, Abessinia and Khartum and a Coasting Voyage from Mombasa to Cape Delgado*, London, 1860

Leonard, A. G., *The Lower Niger and Its Tribes*, London, 1906

Livingstone, David, *Family Letters*, London, Shapera, 1959

Loti, Pierre, *Aziyadé*, Paris, Calmann-Lévy, 1879

Loti, Pierre, *L'Exilée*, Paris, Calmann-Lévy, 1890

Loti, Pierre, *Maroc*, Paris, Calmann-Lévy, 1890

Loti, Pierre, *La Mort de Philae*, Paris, 1909

Lugard, F. J. D., *The Rise of Our East African Empire*, London, 1893

Martinkus-Zemp, Ada, *Européocentrisme et exotisme: l'homme blanc et la femme noire*, in *Cahiers d'Etudes Africaines*, no. 49, 1973

Matteucci, Pellegrino, *In Abissinia*, Milan, Treves, 1880

Massaja, Guglielmo, *In Abissinia e tra i Galla*, Milan, Ariani, 1895

de Maupassant, Guy, *Au Soleil*, Paris, Albin Michel, 1946

Moorehead, Alan, *The White Nile*, Harper and Row, New York, 1960

Naef, Weston J., in coll. with James N. Word, *Era of Exploration: The Rise of Landscape Photography in the American West, 1860–1885*, Boston, 1975

Naipaul, V. S., *A Bend in the River*, New York, Knopf, 1979

Nash, Roderick, *Wilderness and American Mind*, New Haven, Yale University Press, 1967

Oriani, Alfredo, *La lotta politica in Italia. Origini della lotta attuale, 476–1887*, Florence, Della Voce, 1913, Vol. III

Patterson, J. H., *The Man-Eaters of Tsavo, And Other E. African Adventures*, London, 1907

Piscicelli, M., *Nel paese dei Bongo-bongo*, Naples, Dekten e Rocholl, n.d.

Praz, Mario, *The Romantic Agony*, New York, Oxford University Press, 1930

Robecchi-Bricchetti, Luigi, *Nel'Harrar*, Milan, Galli, 1896

Romi, *La conquête du nu*, Paris, n.d.

The Royal Commonwealth Society, *Commonwealth in Focus. 130 Years of Photographic History*, London, 1982

Schiller, Friedrich, *Über naive und sentimentalische Dichtung*, 1795–96. Italian translation, *Sulla poesia ingenua e sentimentale*, Rome, Il Melograno, 1981

Segalen, Victor, *Voix mortes, musique maori*, in *Segalen et Debussy*. Monaco, Editions du Rocher, 1961

Speke, John Hanning, *Journal of the Discovery of the Source of the Nile*, London, 1910

Stanley, Henry M., *The Autobiography of Sir Henry Morton Stanley, G.C.B.* Edited by his wife, Dorothy Stanley, London, n.d.

Stanley, Henry M., *In Darkest Africa*, London, 1890

Thomson, Joseph, *To the Central African Lakes and Back,*
   London, 1881
Zammarano, Vittorio Tedesco, *Alle sorgenti del Nilo Azzurro,*
   Rome, Alfieri & Lacroix, 1919
Zammarano, Vittorio Tedesco, *Azanagó non pianse,* Milan,
   Mondadori, 1939

A Note on the Type

The text of this book was set in a digitized version of Bembo, a well-known Monotype face named for Pietro Bembo, the celebrated Renaissance writer and humanist scholar who was made a cardinal and served as secretary to Pope Leo X. The original cutting of Bembo was made by Francesco Griffo of Bologna only a few years after Columbus discovered America.

Sturdy, well balanced, and finely proportioned, Bembo is a face of rare beauty, extremely legible in all of its sizes.

Composed by
American–Stratford Graphic Services, Inc.,
Brattleboro, Vermont

Printed by
Rembrandt Press,
Milford, Connecticut

Bound by
A. Horowitz & Sons,
Fairfield, New Jersey

Typography and binding design by
Tasha Hall